NEW SONG IN A STRANGE LAND

NEW SONG
in a Strange Land

BY ESTHER WARNER
WITH DECORATIONS BY JO DENDEL

HOUGHTON MIFFLIN COMPANY BOSTON
1948

TO ALL THOSE
who make their life's activities creative.
First, to my parents. Afterwards, to
the Harleys, who create wholeness where
there is disease. Next to Kondea who
saw images in wood, to Poor Boy who
loved the talk of fine cloth to his hand,
to Nya Qua Bee who spoke for his
people, whose book this is.

THERE ARE A NUMBER of persons without whom this book would have been impossible. Two of them are Doctor George Way Harley and his wife, Winifred, of Ganta, Liberia. They gave not only of their time and hospitality, but also of their deep and intelligent understanding of native culture, accumulated during their long years of rich experience in the Hinterland.

Another is Doctor Pearl Hogrefe of the English department of Iowa State College whose belief in sincere and creative expression is responsible for my having attempted to write at all.

Then there is Bob Warner who feels that when Esther wants to try a new creative venture it's his job to help.

Lastly, there are the natives who gave freely of themselves all there is of them in these pages.

To all, I touch my heart in the manner of the Mandingoes and say a deeply felt "Gnasuoh," which in pidgin English is, "thank you, *plenty*."

Contents

New Song
in a Strange Land

A Missy Can't Know

As I approached my house in Liberia for the first time, it looked to me like a giant animal that had crept out of the bush. Against a background of low hills and jungle, it reared high and anticipatory on its front legs, ready to jump. The legs were eight-foot brick piers. There were no vines nor shrubs to bridge the gap between earth and floor. The bricked-in rear crouched low against the ground.

This house-animal had no purring domesticity about it. It might tolerate me, but never would I rule it. This I knew as I walked closer, scuffing my new shoes in the red dust of the road which wound through the rubber trees. My husband had stopped to see his office at Firestone's research building. I had hurried on to our company-built house.

On the concrete steps leading up to what would have been the second floor, had there been any first beneath it, sprawled a lanky black boy wearing white duck trousers and a T-shirt. He was languidly polishing his front teeth with a fuzzed-out stick. Beside him on the steps was a long knife and a black boat-shaped contraption with a

1

curved chimney. He untangled his length and stood up when he saw me, picked up the iron object, leaving the knife on the steps, and saluted.

"Moin, Missy!" he said. "My name Poor Boy. I come to do wash-man work for you. Here my book."

He produced a smudged paper which was a recommendation from a former employer.

"You see," he went on eagerly, "I bring my own iron. I know the work proper, like my book say."

Poor Boy seemed to take it for granted that the matter of his employment was settled. He held the door open for me and I entered a long room, apparently the living room. French windows formed the outside walls. Sixteen empty panes glared at me in the white morning light. Palm fronds brushed the screens. A yellow bird teetered on one of the limbs. It was like being in a tree house. There was the same elation from height, from being on a level with the branches.

The scattered pieces of mission furniture might have belonged in the Ladies' Aid clubroom of a church basement. The floors were highly polished. I could see my elongated reflection stretching unflatteringly across the living room, in the center of which our luggage had been piled in a heap.

It is startling to come suddenly across familiar possessions in entirely new surroundings. It is like meeting an old friend who refuses to recognize you. You see through the tin and wood and leather with the X ray of your packing memories — see the plates swathed in dish towels standing on end in a cardboard box, the empty kerosene lanterns and lamps with extra globes and wicks placed bowl to base in one corner, the new shoes wrapped in tissue paper fitted into the hollows. There is not an unfamiliar object in those cases. But the bright paint on the outside, reading "Monrovia, Liberia, West Africa" is strange. After a while your name begins to look strange, too. It has escaped with your property to the wrong address!

The dusty crates were pathetically small in the big room. They had seemed entirely ample when they sat on the front porch at home. How many bars of soap, how many lipsticks, how many jars of cold cream does a woman use per year? How many buttons does a husband lose from his clothing? How many yards of darning cotton does one darn into how many socks? How many sheets, how many tablecloths, how many napkins wear out? How many hairpins does one lose? How many accessories would it take to make this great bare room livable? And what of accessories for the mind? What would one think about, looking out over the rubber trees toward the jungle?

If you could have only twelve books with which to live for two years, what ones would you choose? That was the question we had asked twenty-five of the best-read persons we knew. The answers read like a list of what one *ought* to read, but never does. The books which had finally found their way into the boxes were art books for me and botany books for my husband. The ought-to-reads lost out.

Each of us had come to Liberia with his own purposes and expectancies. I think my own life in Africa really began when I was a small girl on an Iowa farm. When

I carried coffee to my father in the field, I tried to meet him on the crest of the highest hill. After he had gone on down the furrow, I sat on the warm earth and looked down the straight rows until they merged in the distance. They carried me to the horizon. I thought that if I could really stand there, I could send my thoughts on to the next horizon, spanning the earth in giant stride.

When I told my mother about this, she spread a map of the world on the kitchen table and read aloud from it the strange-sounding names of far places. The *Grain Coast*, the *Ivory Coast*, the *Gold Coast*, the *Congo*, the *Bight of Benin!* My mother was taking me on my first trip down the West Coast before I could read. The colors on the map seemed to go with the names of the places. Green and gold and ivory and black had fused in my mind like glowing gems, while I crossed the Atlantic, hand over hand, on the tightwire of the Equator and hopped onto land a few spots of color below Liberia. After this vision of the world spread out on paper, I made up songs to go with the names of the places I would visit. *Bight of Benin* was just right to go with a long step, a hop, and a jump.

The next time I heard *Bight of Benin* put into song was aboard the blacked-out ship which carried me to the fulfillment of the old dream.

> Beware! Beware! The Bight of Benin!
> Forty come out; thirty-nine stay in.

It is an old sailors' chantey which originated when West Africa well deserved to be called the "white man's graveyard."

Now I stood in the middle of the living room of the house which was to be my home on the Firestone rubber plantation, where my husband was to work as research botanist. I was in Africa, I had apparently acquired my first servant, and I stood fretting about the puny contents of some packing cases! Here was a continent, or at least a country, to be discovered and I was filled with woman-ish worry.

What I actually knew about Liberia was very little. What I hoped to discover about primitive carvings and native handicrafts was a lot. I knew that Monrovia was the capital. I had seen briefly this desolate village of cor-rugated iron, decaying wood, and mud huts when we disembarked. I knew that the area of the country was about that of the state of Ohio, that back in 1820 our government had helped sponsor a colony of freed slaves on the coast, that the descendants of these people were the Liberians (or "Americo-Liberians"), and that they governed through a so-called democracy the native tribes-men whose history is lost in myth. Set down like an irregular yellow patch on an almost blank map, sprinkled with words such as "unexplored," "forests," "elephants" was the Firestone plantation. It was the size of a large midwestern county, thirty crooked miles inland from Monrovia. Dotted around the plantation were the com-pany-built houses where about a hundred and twenty-five white men and perhaps forty wives lived with as many comforts as they could transplant from home.

Much more important to me than these sketchy bits of information was the fact that some of the finest carved ritual masks I had seen came from the interior of Liberia, and that Doctor Harley, the man who knew most about them, was at a mission on the interior boundary. I had seen some of these masks while I was studying sculpture at Columbia University. After my first glimpse of them, I had felt that I must, someday, get to their source. I knew that life in the villages along the jungle paths went on much as it had before the colony of Liberians was planted on the coast. This meant a handicraft culture to be studied and explored. But for the moment, exploration could start with the house which was to shelter me between expeditions.

"Come on, Poor Boy. Let's see the house." He had stood silently while I contemplated the luggage. Poor Boy could absent himself in spirit so completely while one was lost in reverie that his physical presence seemed to have vanished as well. But when one thought of him again or needed him, he was *there*.

Two bedrooms with a bath between made up the sleeping quarters. Above each bed swung a square frame hung from the ceiling with chains. Draped over the frames were clouds of snowy mosquito netting.

In the bathroom a small boy was standing almost on his head scrubbing the floor of the shower.

"This my country brother, Johnny," explained Poor Boy. "I think you can like him for a steward boy. He carries fine book."

Johnny straightened up and grinned. He was slight of body and large of head. His features had a plastic quality which put them at the mercy of his moods. From the tooth-gleaming grin his face drew into an anxious wedge.

"Moin, Missy! I make everything proper?"

"Clean," I said.

"But, Missy, I need small something."

"What do you need?"

"*Medicine*, Missy! Medicine for the W.C."

"The Missy buy some at the Trading Company," Poor Boy said. "I see some live in the case in the kitchen just now." He disappeared and came back with a can of Sani-Flush.

Back of a towel rack two wirelike affairs about two inches long twitched between the metal and the wall.

"What's that?" I asked as calmly as possible.

"Cockroach hands." Poor Boy was nonchalant. "There is medicine for them too. But every day, Johnny will look for eggs. See?" He plucked something that looked like a vitamin capsule out of a fold in the shower curtain. "Plenty cockroach babies come from these. When they grow big, they fly through the house like birds."

"Missy," Johnny said, still anxious, "how is it that you buy only small-small at the Trading Company?"

I thought I had bought a mountain of supplies, enough for a month. We passed through a long hall to the kitchen.

"Even the medicine is not sufficient," [1] Johnny muttered, as he walked along behind me. "No medicine for the sink, no burned-pan medicine. And the chop! People will eat all in one night and nothing will remain for the next day."

"There are only two of us, Johnny."

[1] Native system of comparison: *small-small, small, sufficient, plenty, hellova.*

"But, ah! You don't know, Missy, how many people will come to sit down at table. Fifteen can come, one time."

"I haven't asked anyone to dinner." I was definitely on the defensive now.

"You do' *ask* people to dinner. If you *ask* them, that is a party. People just come for dinner. You hear the motorcar. They come up the steps. You say, 'What you like to drink?' After, you say, 'How-do.' More people come. You say more-again, 'What-you-like-to-drink-how-do.' Chop time come. I count the people and go tell the cook how many. I dress the table. Then I say, 'Chop ready, Missy,' and all the people sit down at table. That is everyday palaver. When you tire for this, you go sit down on someone else. But it is not good to sit down on a bachelor. They don't take care for good chop."

In the kitchen a boy with no shirt and trousers the color of his smoky-looking skin stirred something in an iron pot on the roaring wood stove. Just under his nose, a hunk of charcoal glowed in a clay pipe. In the dirty sink lay a knife, two feet long. The walls were smoke-stained and big cobwebs festooned with soot swung from the corners.

"How you can cook boy-chop in the Missy kitchen?" The immaculate Johnny avoided touching any of the tables or furniture. Then to me, "This is Sammi, Missy. He like to cook for you."

"A steward boy is not chief in the kitchen," Sammi looked scornfully at Johnny. "In the kitchen the cook is the chief and it is not for a small-boy steward boy to tell him something. How-do, Missy?" It seemed I was just an afterthought.

It didn't look as though I were going to be chief in any part of the house. I walked over to the stove and looked in the bubbling pot. In some greasy water, two frogs which had been neither drawn nor quartered tossed in a boil.

"This kitchen is very dirty," I said in my best Iowa-State-College-home-economics voice. "If you are going to cook for me, you must clean all the walls and make everything spotless. You will not cook any more frogs unless you take the insides out first. And" — seeing that the box of stovewood was fine mahogany — "you must not burn any more of this fine wood. I want it for carving."

Sammi was amazed. He considered all of these mandates and took them up in order.

"Cleaning the kitchen is yardboy work, Missy. It is not for cook man to clean walls! My frogs I will cook in the boys' kitchen, but the insides must not come out. White person throw the best of the meat away. About the wood, I do not understand, but plenty more, same good wood live under the house. Plenty there!

"And now, Missy, I need one hellova big kettel for boil water. You bring some?"

"I will see." (The biggest kettle I had brought was a large saucepan.) "Now tell me this, Sammi, *do you know how to cook?*"

"Yeah, Missy, I know." He looked somewhat insulted. "First *I will tell you how to cook water.* To cook water is necessary. The last Missy to stay for this house lack small to die in the hospital from belly-runs. The water must sit down on the stove for long time but it must roll in vex the time I cover on the timepiece with my hand." He spanned thirty minutes with his knobby fingers on an old watch that hung by his side.

"But that clock doesn't run, Sammi." There was no back on the empty case.

"No, Missy, it is like the frog, the inside is the best part and it is gone. Now the time die-o."

"I have a clock in the packing cases."

Sammi's face lighted up. "Maybe it is the kind where the time die every night and you make it live again with a key?

"All right, now I will tell you how to make bread, Missy."

"There was no yeast at the Trading Company, so we can't make bread."

"Oh, that's all right, Missy. This is the one we can do. The people in the camp catch the palm wine from the palm tree in the bush. The tree-water run from hole in the tree into so-so country gourd. It stay there until it is full of frisky. Sometime the monkey find it and drink all before the people come. Then the monkey frisky too much. Sometime the people drink the wine before they reach camp and then they happy too much, but the Missy not glad when no bread live for the house. When I catch the wine for the Missy I put small flour, small sugar, small Crisco inside, and it sleep all night for the kitchen. He grow big like woman with pickin in the belly the time while he sleep. Soon morning, I put more flour inside, I beat him softly-softly with my hand. The bread, he can be fine when the palm wine be new, but if the palm wine be old, he can't grow big belly on the dough. Better you give me measure of flour and I look for the palm wine."

I opened the sack to measure the flour and saw that particles of it were jumping in a lively manner.

"We can't use this," I exclaimed. "It's alive with bugs."

Sammi laughed. "The flour, he always alive," he said. "You sift the bugs out. After, if you see in your bread some bug that has gone over the edge of the sieve, you can't care too much. All the new Missy make palaver for bugs first time, but after, they don't care."

I did not answer, but I was not going to cease caring!

"I will send to the market for some coffee," Sammi went on. "Now I will tell you how I must do with the coffee."

"Every morning when the fire is small, I put the coffee there for that day. After, I beat him in the mortar. Now, Missy, you like me to tell you how to cook any more things?"

I thought I'd had enough instruction for one day. I looked over the three boys who seemed to have hired themselves to me. Poor Boy was the unobtrusive dreamy one. Johnny was the worry-wart, too concerned about everything, especially his own appearance. Sammi was cocksure and truculent and would be the most difficult to manage. Neither Johnny nor Sammi seemed to think I knew anything about keeping a house, and this was dis-concerting. Poor Boy had not cast any aspersions and I turned to him as a sort of ally.

"Is that thing in your hand an iron, Poor Boy?"

"Yes, Missy. I will show you how I use it." He swung the top open. It was hollow inside. "This place I put the hot charcoal. But first, I make the charcoal.

"I know charcoal palaver plenty, Missy. First, I look for the hard, hard stick in the bush. Then I look for big bug-a-bug hill like that one." He pointed at a huge ter-mite mound at the back of the yard. It was cone-shaped and higher than my head. "I take so-so hand shovel, and make big room inside the bug-a-bug bungalow. Ah, hah! this vex the bug-a-bug plenty-o, but I can't fear bug-a-bug. Sometime, I will see the Queen, and I will chop her, one time." He smacked his lips, and a hungry gleam appeared in his eyes.

"After I fini dig, I lay the stick inside, so." He crossed his fingers to demonstrate. "Then I lay small stick across the door, and I plaster all with mud, save for small hole in the bottom part and small hole in the top part. Then

I put fire there and leff it. When the charcoal come out, it can be fine-o.

"When I iron clothes, I light small charcoal and put him inside. When the iron be plenty hot, I iron the strong clothes, when the fire lack small to die-o, I iron the Missy-clothes that shine.

"Also, I know starch palaver, Missy. I chop the cassava fine on one so-so iron with plenty nail-holes to make it catch the cassava hard. Then I carry it for the bamboo mat and lay it in the sun. After, I wash it, wash it, with water, the sun carry the water, and fine dry starch remain."

As I walked out of my house past the shiny electric refrigerator, past the mission furniture, past the beds with spun-rubber mattresses, and looked out at the swamp from the piazza, time seemed telescoped, fore and aft, and I felt confused about where I stood in the groove of centuries. The swamps were rank and primeval. One might almost expect a dinosaur to raise his long neck out of the huge ferns. In the labor camp beside the swamp lived a people who ate with their hands and boiled bull-frogs without cleaning them, people who had progressed as far as smelting crude iron from the rocks when the first white people found them. The living-room furniture brought us to 1900. The refrigerator, the plumbing, the electric lights, and the house with its concrete and brick and simple horizontal lines were of today. I knew that I would have to reconcile myself to these disparities before I could live my days without confusion.

The next day when I was in the kitchen, where Sammi managed in a subtle way to make me feel like an intruder,

I noticed that his hands were laid open in great festered cracks. Quite against his will, I sent him to the Company hospital.

Maybe it's leprosy, I thought, and forbade him to come into the house or touch the doorknobs until we knew what it was.

Toward evening he came back with a note from one of the native dressers. It read:

> Dear Mrs. Warner,
>
>   Your boy is suffering from craw-craw. It is a disease those get who don't wash sufficient. It is necessary to use plenty blue soap. Then craw-craw can finish one time.
>
>   Yours dresser,
>
>   George F. Kennedy

I distributed pieces of blue soap and delivered what I thought was an eloquent lecture on cleanliness.

"The next person that gets craw-craw I will sack," I said.

The next day my husband had a rash of angry-looking blisters on his hand.

"I have got craw-craw," he said, when he came home from the hospital. Johnny gulped and ran out of the room with his hand over his mouth. I sank into a chair. Johnny's laugh exploded into a treble cackle as soon as he shut the door. He was soon calling all the boys under the house, telling them the fine joke.

That evening I heard their dishwashing song:

> Craw-craw catch the boss, craw-craw catch the boss.
> Missy have to sack the boss, Ohah! ohah! ohah!

In the days that followed, it was often a question of

whether I was managing the boys or they were managing us.

There was the matter of the waxed floor, for instance. It had been polished until it was a hazard. Every morning all the furniture was carried out on the piazza. Then Buno yardboy came upstairs with a Kpuesi drum under his arm. It was about a foot long and made of hollow wood the shape of an hourglass with monkey skin stretched across both ends. A set of raffia strings connected the skins on either end, and by pressing these strings between the arm and the body, changes in pitch were effected. Both boys tied old bed blankets on their feet, and while Buno thumped the underarm drum, they danced wildly over every inch of the floor. The drum increased in vigor as they gathered momentum, singing a "floor-shine song" at the tops of their voices.

When I said that such drastic measures were not necessary every day and the floor "shine too much," Johnny looked thoughtful.

"Well, Missy, I tell you," he said, "Better we shine the floor small-small every day. Else dust can live under the chair and when Missy's goo' friends come, the steward boy can feel shame."

The wild floor dance continued daily, but it was not small.

When my husband brought home our first pet, a little zebra antelope indigenous only to Liberia, I was sure he would break his pencil-slim legs even if we did not. His pretty little hoofs skidded on the smooth wood until he stood with all four legs scooted out at an awkward bracing angle and looked at me from enormous eyes which seemed to say, "How about rescuing me from this outlandish situation?" But when I moved toward him to pick him up, he leaped on the sofa, slitting the upholstery with the edges of his hoofs.

"Missy," Johnny said, "that Small Meat tell me something."

"What thing he tell you, Johnny?"

"Well, Missy, he say, 'I fear this place, yah. I beg you tell Missy I like my own small bungalow under the house.'"

Small Meat went to live under the house and the floor continued to glisten.

I decided to curtain my windows with the native blue-and-white-striped country cloth, adding a curtain at a time as I was able to find it for sale. Each one would be a little different, but all of them would be similar. It was difficult to make the country cloth hang straight because the native looms have no device for keeping warp tension even. I sewed and resewed the narrow strips together on the first curtain. Johnny watched me with a troubled look. Finally, he said, "Missy, I want to tell you country story."

I was glad to stop sewing and listen.

"First time, the baboon was born, he was fine, fine baby. His ma look at him and she see he fine, only thing, she thought her fine baby have awkward mouth. So, she say, 'All right, let me fix the mouth part.'

"She fix, she fix, she fix, ti' she spoil it. Then she say, 'Oh, let me fix it more.' So she spoil it more.

"Now people look at the baboon. They see the awkward mouth that is past all fix palaver.

"When someone fix something too much, the people say, 'Leff it, yah. Too much fix can spoil fine thing.'"

I "leff" the curtain. After all, it didn't look too bad.

Sammi Cook and I had one of our many differences of opinion about the proper way to cook shrimp, which the natives call crawfish.

A Kpuesi man named Ga-ga brought them in an old calabash every morning. Ga-ga is the Kpuesi name for duck. The appellation fitted him well. He had a shovel-billed mouth which parted in an indignant quack if the shrimp were dead and I refused to buy them.

He counted out the olive-green flopping creatures, "three-for-one-cent, three-for-one-cent," placing a pebble on the step every time he succeeded in getting three of them into the enamel pan which Sammi held out to receive them. In the end he must have as many ha'pennies as there were pebbles on the step, plus "one more again" put there for his *dash,* while he added an extra shrimp for my dash. Then he waddled off to a bachelor's house "where no Missy sit down to take care for all the small-small thing" to sell the dead ones which I had refused.

The shrimp were to be cooked in the manner of lobster, dropped one at a time into violently boiling water. I had discussed this in detail with Sammi.

"Yeah, Missy, I know that one," he had said.

But when I stepped into the kitchen, I saw that the shrimp had been put on the stove in cold water and were protesting vigorously against the growing heat. When I took the lid off the kettle, one of them jumped out on the hot stove and looked at me with what might have been reproach from his black-bead eyes.

I was revolted and furious. I had no need to "throw a vex" (the art of pretending great anger for the sake of discipline, without really being in inner turmoil). My vex was real.

Sammi was puzzled. He picked a small stick out of the woodbox and put it into the stove.

"Look, Missy," he said. "I put wood to the fire, and you no vex. The crawfish part be the same palaver."

"Bwaho!" I said. "When you put your hand to the hot stove, that palaver and the crawfish palaver be the same one."

He shook his head sadly. White people had such queer ideas!

We tangled again over the matter of rice. I smelled it burning and went to the kitchen to investigate.

"You must use a big kettle, and plenty, plenty water," I said.

"Oh, no, Missy. That way, the rice can stick together. When I use small water and waste and burn the bottom part, then the top part can be dry and fine too much."

"Look, Sammi," I said. "In the United States, I go to one school called a college. I sit down there the time of four rice-plantings. There I study the whole time the sewing palaver, the cooking palaver, the keep-house palaver. *And the big school say the rice be cooked with plenty water.*"

"Missy," Sammi said sadly, "it true you sew fine. You tailor past [better than] all the people. You tailor past Ashmanah, self. But a Missy can't know our-part rice palaver. Tonight, chop time, you try the rice. If you find the rice be fine-o, you must agree for my way. But if the rice no be fine, then I agree for the one the school say."

The rice was swollen into great separate kernels that were dry and delicious. I had never eaten finer rice. We said no more about the way to cook it.

CHAPTER TWO

Guinea Grain

O<small>UR</small> F<small>IRESTONE HOUSE</small> was in Liberia, but not of it. It was an island of transplanted America. The labor camp near-by was not typically Liberian either. In the village of three or four hundred natives, those of different tribes, who would not dare to cross each other's territories alone, lived in adjacent huts. The plantation was a sort of melting pot of tribesmen. Scattered through the unplanted areas were a few villages whose land had not yet been claimed for planting. In one of these lived Chief Ashmanah, a Mandingo renowned for his tailoring.

I had brought a bolt of white duck for servants' uniforms which I planned to make myself. Johnny was aghast at the idea and finally implied that nothing but man tailoring would do justice to the fine cloth. Sammi was indifferent to uniforms. It would be one-more-again-thing to keep clean. Oh, he would like a big cook cap like the one he'd seen on a Cream of Wheat box, but that was enough. He was proper in shorts and a cap! Jackets were hot and kept a man from toweling up the sweat (with the dish towel, I supposed) that ran like a river down his belly when he stood over the stove.

Poor Boy was quietly grateful at the prospect of a new
suit and suggested we carry the cloth to Ashmanah.

We set off with Poor Boy in the lead, carrying the
material on his head and a big knife in his hand. The
morning was cool with the feeling that it was going to
be warm.

I was cold and hot at the same time. Every leaf and
blade of grass was shimmering wet and beginning to
steam. Bright fungi grew everywhere.

Suddenly Poor Boy stopped short.

"Take care, Missy! Driver!"

A black moving ribbon of ants, two inches wide,
crossed our path. They came out of the bush on one side
and entered it again on the other. Rows of soldier ants
lined each side of the ribbon. In the center the black
mass flowed viscously.

"Sometimes they take three days to pass," said Poor
Boy, "and if one ever bites you, you will feel one hellova
fire!"

The Mandingo village was a clearing in the jungle
along a stream. There were clumps of banana trees behind the dozen mud huts. The earth in the compound
was hard-packed and swept. The drumlike thump we
had heard came from the rice-beating in the center of the
compound. Two women worked at each mortar, a fire-
hollowed log about three feet high, old and beautifully
carved. Each woman held a pole which she rammed in
her turn into the mouth of the mortar. Then she held
her pole high while the woman facing her did the same.
A shrill song kept the rhythm, and the flying sticks never
collided or splashed grain out of the mortars. The

women were naked above the waist and their pendulous breasts flew out at right angles to their torsos and snapped back with force at every plunge of the poles.

"One mortar Missy must buy," Poor Boy said. "You must have a new one that the boys don't use. It's for more things than the rice. You grind the coffee, and make peanut butter out of ground-peas [peanuts], and beat cassava, and loosen the pulp on palm nuts for country chop, and more besides, in the mortar. For your-part, it must always be washed first with filtered water. Otherwise, white person can get belly-runs."

The women beating rice paid no attention as I passed to the largest hut. Ashmanah lay in a purple string hammock stretched between the porch poles of the chief's

house. He unfolded his gaunt length joint by joint and
stood up. He wore a red fez on his head and was draped
in a loose burnoose of blue-and-white-striped cloth. Beneath the flowing robe a pair of baggy trousers ballooned
around his ankles and brushed the tops of his heelless
red slippers. His nose and hands were remarkably long
and thin, covered with tightly drawn gray skin. There
was a great dignity in Ashmanah. I had known it even
when he lay in his hammock.

"*Salaam aleikum* [Peace be with you]," he greeted us,
and bowed.

"*Aleikum a salaam*," returned Poor Boy. "This one
new Missy, fresh from the United States. She like to see
your house and your town."

"How do to the new Missy!" Ashmanah reached out
his hand. The handshake ended by his snapping the
middle finger of his hand against my middle finger. The
snap was a feeble click because I was unprepared for it.

Poor Boy laughed. "Look, Missy, we will show you
the country handshake." He took Ashmanah's hand and
their fingers parted with a joint-rattling pop.

"Goo'-goo' friends snap fingers several times," Poor
Boy went on. "If you like someone small, small, you
snap fingers one time."

"Come, I show you my house," invited Ashmanah.

There are many ways to open a door to a stranger.
There is the notched and grudging progress of a door
opened on hinges of suspicion, the nervous haste of an
insincerely opened door, the cringing progress when
apologies are to follow. Ashmanah flung open his heavy

door with a welcoming gesture that ended with his fingertips on his heart. There was graciousness as well as
dignity in Ashmanah.

The bareness of the hut did not make it poor. The
newly swept look of everything made it the abode of
asceticism rather than of poverty. A folded country cloth
lay across the foot of a crude bed covered with a bamboo
mat. A wooden box sat at the foot of the bed. In it were
three enamel pans, a clay pot, and a small blue enamel
teakettle. Under the bed was a small wooden trunk.
Ashmanah pulled it out and showed us several lengths
of country cloth. They were woven in narrow strips of
coarse, creamy cotton thread. The rough texture, the
natural cotton color, and the decorative way the strips
had been sewed together with an overhand stitch was
most attractive.

"That's what I want for my curtains," I said. "Do your
people make cloth like this, Ashmanah?"

"No, Missy, Mandingo man can't make cloth. The Vai
people, the Buzi people make fine cloth. Mandingo man
carry the cloth and sell them."

"Will you sell this one?" It was large as a bed sheet
and would curtain two French doors.

"I no sell this one: I buy him, Missy. This one my
bed blanket. But I look for one more again for your
part."

"Is this all a chief requires to keep house?" I asked in
amazement when we had seen everything in the hut.

Ashmanah answered, "We-part can't need plenty
thing. White people see plenty trouble for all the differ-
ent-different thing he need. It not so?"

"Yes," I said, "that is true."

"Mandingo man carry plenty cargo in his heart," Ash-manah said, "and when he need small something, God give him sense to go for the bush and put eye on the small thing he need."

"I would like to learn some of the things God gives you sense to see in the bush, Ashmanah," I said.

"Well, Missy, you see, plenty thing stay in the bush," explained Ashmanah, "but person can't learn plenty thing one time [at once]. God talk softly-softly, one-one."

We inspected the village. A new baby had been born in the night to one of Ashmanah's wives. He looked glum when he told us about it.

"Pickin out of that woman die every time," he said.

The mother sat in front of her hut on a bamboo mat, bathing the tiny wrinkled baby in a white-enameled pan. She scooped water in her palm from beside the little clay-daubed body and poured it into the child's mouth.

"That child should not drink bath water," I said in my best child-care and -training manner.

"Only pepper and small medicine to make pickin strong inside the water," said Ashmanah. "So our people do every time. Pickin out of that woman can't live."

"The pickin must chop milk from the mother. Bath water is not fit pickin-chop." I knelt on the mat and pushed the child's mouth over the nipple of one of the woman's swollen breasts to be sure they understood. The woman snatched her breast angrily from the child.

"Only the water with medicine inside for three days," said Ashmanah. "So is the way of our people."

"You make Death the way of your people!"

"No," argued Ashmanah. "When God say 'live,' my
pickin live. You see Mohammedan, my fine boy? Soon-
time he can go for French side, learn the Mohammedan
book proper. God agree for Mohammedan. Already, he
talk French and write Arabic."

Mohammedan sat cross-legged on the piazza of a hut,
writing beautiful Arabic characters on a wooden slate
with a feather which he dipped into red ink in a little
clay pot. A neat margin, widest at the bottom, framed
the rust-red characters on the gray wood. Mohammedan
was dressed like his father except that his robe was shorter and he was not wearing the bulky pantaloons beneath
it. The remarkable thing about Mohammedan was the
brightness of his eyes. They were big and ran about
under his long lashes as though his thoughts were chas-
ing them.

He showed us the slate proudly.

"What does it say?" I asked.

"Truth from the Allah-book," he said. "When I go for the French side, I learn the meaning."

"You mean that you can't read what you write."

"I read small [a little] Missy, but when the war finish, that time I learn the book proper. War can't wait for people to sit down easy, learn book." His eyes chased merrily from corner to corner. "Plenty thing wait for Mohammedan to learn."

"Would you like to learn to read English, Mohammedan? If you like, I can teach you. Then you will show me some of the things you know about the bush."

Mohammedan hesitated. "Well, Missy," he said finally, "it is good to learn to read your-part book, but *God talks in Arabic,* and I want to hear the one God says."

I did not think that Mohammedan or Ashmanah would like to hear that I had an English translation of the Koran. They might believe that God speaks in the thunder but they would not admit of the English language as a fitting vehicle for his thoughts.

"Mohammedan," explained Poor Boy, "the new Missy like to learn plenty bush palaver. Tomorrow-time you come for our house, you stay with the Missy. The flower in the bush, the medicine for writing, all the plenty thing you show the new Missy, yah?"

"Soon morning," agreed Mohammedan.

"You see," said Ashmanah stubbornly. "Mohammedan, fine boy. All my pickin from Mohammedan's ma can live. All the pickin from the other woman can die."

In front of a hut a woman was feeding rice to a small child. She crouched on the dirt sill and spread her legs wide, making a table of her skirt where the child lay. One hand acted as a funnel to the child's mouth. The other formed rice in balls and with the index finger working like a ramrod, she forced food into the squirming child's mouth. Ball after ball of rice was poked into the wriggling infant.

"That baby is too small to eat solid food," I said.

"The woman's milk is finished," Ashmanah explained. He scornfully flipped one of the shriveled dugs that swung against her gaunt ribs to show how worthless her breasts had become. They resembled empty pocketbooks of cracked old leather from which all bounty had long since been drained.

Another woman held a baby at arm's length while

nature asserted its requirements. She swept dust over the fouled earth with a twig brush and laid the child on its stomach across her lap while a mangy dog came and thoroughly licked the child clean.

"Dog is the black baby's toilet paper," Poor Boy explained.

On the edge of the town, a woman was shaking little golden seeds out of brown pods into a basket.

"Sesame!" I exclaimed. Bob had learned to like it very much in Syria. "Can I buy some, Ashmanah?"

"I sorry too much, Missy, but we no got plenty." Ashmanah looked convincingly sorry. "Sometime you can see some in the market. I look for the seed for you."

"How do you people use it?" I asked.

"*Fu-fu!*" he exclaimed. "That woman yonder that beat cassava in the mortar just now make fu-fu."

The cassava had been cooked, and after she had beaten it into a dough she took it out of the mortar and placed it on a flat basket which they called a "fanner." Then more of a cassava went into the mortar to be pounded.

"We make a soup to go with it and put the sesame seed into the soup," Ashmanah said. "Sometimes white man can like it, but it is work to eat. It fights the teeth."

Half a dozen women approached from the creek, their heads piled high with bamboo fish traps. Babies were tied against their backs, inside their wrap-around skirts. The babies' heads jerked with the mothers' steps, rolling on their necks like little black cannon balls.

Poor Boy indicated an ugly, scrawny light-skinned lad in the procession who cringed when anyone looked at him.

"That small-boy's name be Missy," Poor Boy told me.

"Why Missy?" He was obviously a boy.

"Because if his white-man pa had keep his own white woman on the plantation, that pickin would never been born. His ma was a fine black Mandingo woman. But that boy be nothing. He not white, he not black, he nothing."

"And," Ashmanah added glumly, "that Missy' pa paid me no money for the woman. It was altogether bad."

"How many women do you keep, Ashmanah?" I asked.

"Not sufficient to plant the new rice," said Ashmanah sadly. "You see, I owe plenty money, I can't pay this time. I borrow the money to pay the government my hut tax. So it is necessary I pawn women for debt; otherwise, I would live for jail already. Now only few, maybe twenty, remain. I do' know how I can manage for the rice palaver."

"You can't make farm yourself, Ashmanah?"

"Oh, no, Missy. A chief can't scratch farm. And the rice is woman-part work. Rice from a man's hand can't grow. Can a man born pickin? No more can he grow rice. I tailor shirts to get money but it take plenty sew-shirt to redeem one woman. I do' know how I can manage for the rice palaver. I pay twelve pounds for a woman, and for the lack of the hut tax and three pounds one man with hard ways hold me, it is necessary I pawn her."

"And when you pawn a woman and she goes to live with the man you owe — who gets the children if they have babies?" I asked.

"They belong to the pa. Otherwise, I could make more babies for my village."

"Then if you get money, you can redeem the woman?"

"Sometimes, but if the man who take her owe some other man, he can pawn her again. Plenty men can take her this way. So if the money don't get to the hand of the last man who have her, I can't get the woman again. It is *hard for a man* to have to pawn a woman!"

Mohammedan walked out of the town with us. At the waterside several women up to their waists in water were skimming the creek with raffia seines. One woman lay

on the bank moaning. I stopped to look at her. Her eyes
rolled back and foam showed on her lips. Her abdomen
was distended. No one showed any interest in her plight.

"What is wrong with the woman?" I was concerned.

"I can no say, Missy," evaded Mohammedan. "Sometimes, some bad medicine can catch her."

"I think I could send her to the hospital."

"Oh, no, Missy!" Mohammedan seemed alarmed.
"God agree for the woman to die."

I saw no way to intervene with Allah.

"Missy," Poor Boy told me later, "I think poison catch
that woman. The Mandingos are clever with poison."

"But I thought one Mohammedan could not kill
another."

"It is a woman, Missy," Poor Boy said gently. "It is
easy for a woman to have knives turn in her heart against
another woman. Men fight with cutlass, but not so a
woman. Poison is the woman-way."

Mohammedan turned beyond the creek and whistled
like a bird. A small naked boy with a raffia basket on his
head ran down to the waterside. He gave the basket to
Mohammedan who gave it to me. It was full of sesame
seed.

"Dash for the new Missy," said Mohammedan. "Ashmanah say he like the new Missy's heart to lie down good
in the country. Tomorrow I come show you how we-part
make country ink. *That part*, country medicine, God
agree for white man to know."

Mohammedan was on hand early in the morning to
guide me to the top of Mount Cryan, which is the high-

est point on the plantation. It is not much of a mountain as far as height is concerned. The fame is in its
sacredness as an old stamping ground for a powerful
Kpuesi devil or spirit, and in the occasional bush cow
who comes down off its height to charge the tapping boys
as they collect latex.

What I saw after hours of tortuous climbing during
which saw grass laced through my shoes and tree thorns
clawed my clothing, was neither devil nor bush cow. It
was the history of Liberia spun across the petals of a pepper flower.

At first, I mistook the pepper blossoms for orchids.

They grew close to the ground beneath stalks of glossy leaves about three feet high. Some of the flowers had matured into scarlet seed pods, four or five inches long. Mohammedan gathered the flowers for me and the pods for himself. There were black seeds inside the rosy rind, and he chewed these as we climbed. During one of our pauses for breath, he showed me that the glossy leaf stock and the flowers came off the same horizontal-growing root. I had made no connection between foliage and flower.

When we were on top of Mount Cryan, Mohammedan whacked away enough of the low bush so I could look out over the plantation for many miles in several directions. Then he sat down cross-legged on a rock and told me about pepper — and history.

Legends, as well as certain words of European languages, persist among the natives with surprising accuracy considering the lack of manuscript to preserve them. Later, when I checked Mohammedan's story, I found it essentially correct.

"This one," said Mohammedan, picking up the delicate white blossom, tinged with pink, "be black man's trouble."

"How so?" I asked.

"His name be pepper," said Mohammedan, as though that ought to explain everything.

I was not an informed listener. Even if he had called it "Malaaguetta pepper," or "grains of paradise," or "Guinea grain," its significance would have been lost on me then. Now I know that the grain coast has its name from these guinea grains. I urged him to go on.

"First time, long ago," said Mohammedan, "no white person humbug black people. All we black. No trouble."

(Actually, the Mandingos are supposed to have descended from the Fulas to the northward, who it is thought are semi-Caucasian. They consider themselves black, however, even though they are taller than the other natives and less Negroid in feature.)

"All right," Mohammedan went on, "some white people across the big water get hungry in the heart for gold. They come here, they look, they look. They find small. So they never humbug plenty for gold. But ah hah! They find this one, the pepper. They put him on the tongue. They like.

"Then they carry the pepper to their big white woman chief [that was Queen Elizabeth]. She like him plenty. When she drink their part cane-juice [brewed beer] she like plenty pepper inside. So she send plenty men, plenty ship to carry pepper.

"When the white man come for pepper, he see that the back of the black man is strong to carry load. All right! He carry black man also. Soon he leave the pepper entirely and carry only the strong black man to do his work.

"There!" Mohammedan pointed out through the clearing toward Cape Mount.

"Plenty black man get eaten up in the belly of white man's ship there.

"Long time pass. All the long time the black man get caught and go from here. Plenty-plenty go.

"Some white man in your country see it be bad thing. They say, 'All right, let us send some back.' So they do.

"The black man that came back sit down there." He pointed toward Monrovia.

"They sit down under the big tree on Providence Island. You have seen that small island by the waterside, Ma. They talk big palaver.

"From the white man's country they bring some so-so black pots, some brass bars, some American cloth, some other small-small thing. They give these to old Chief Peter.

"They say, 'We want to live here, make farm.' The chief say, 'All right, we left [let] you. Sit down here.'

"They sit down. The people who never left here see that these United States black people get white ways in the United States. They act big-man. But they talk soft. They say to more and more chiefs, 'Take cargo. Give us land.'

"Now, Ma, these people be the government people. They got the whole country. All we got to live under two laws. We got to live under the Liberian government law. They got plenty soldier. We don't give our heart to that law. The other law is the law of our people where the chief is the big man. That one we give heart to.

"So you see, Ma," he said, bruising the wilted pepper blossom in his fingers, "this one bring plenty trouble. First it bring the white man, who carry the black man. Then black man with white-man-ways come here and take our land. I eat this flower seed because it help when I thirsty. But it tell we something also. The something it talk is this: There is a thirsty that is not for the belly. There is a thirsty for land that belong to we."

He threw the pepper blossom to the ground and

looked out over the distance. Was he surveying his inheritance?

The Mandingos have the black man's patience. But they also have the black man's keen sense of justice. They are "by the ears with the Prophet." They know what he said about vengeance.

CHAPTER THREE

Peaches and Doilies

I HAD WALKED to my neighbor's house for the stated purpose of borrowing some coffee. I might have sent a boy with a note, but I wanted to talk with a woman. With the exception of two or three groups of houses, the staff residences are spread out over the plantation, four or five miles apart, one on each division, in order that each planter may live near his native labor village. The plantation women saw surprisingly little of one another, except at the Club where conversation did not run to housekeeping problems.

While I was making small-talk with my hostess, her cook came in to ask for salt. She rose wearily and fingered through a huge bunch of keys in her pocket.

"I get so tired of keys, of locking and unlocking doors," she said. "And people at home ask me what I do with my time when I have so many servants. I could do a washing every week in the time I spend hunting for keys and counting things."

"Couldn't you make one of the boys responsible, so that you wouldn't need to lock everything?" I asked.

"We do have them all under bond. But unless you

actually catch a boy with stolen goods, you cannot accuse
him or you will get sued and the judge will be an Americo-Liberian lawyer. It is hard to be a foreigner."

"I suppose," I said, "that it seems to them that we have
so much and they have so little."

"The strange thing about it," she mused, "is that theft
is almost unknown in the interior. It is when the natives
come in contact with 'civilization' that they learn to steal.
You have to expect a squeeze. You count it as part of
your cost of living. But unless you watch it, the squeeze
becomes a chute leading from the kitchen to the camp. I
guess I'm in a bad mood this morning. I don't know
whether I'm getting fever again or whether it's a hang-
over. Or maybe I'm homesick. There hasn't been any
mail for so long."

She went to the window and looked out toward the
coast. She seemed small and fragile standing against the
brightness of the big French doors. I knew she had forgotten my presence.

I looked around the room while I waited for her to
speak again. In addition to the regular company-pro-
vided furniture, there were some nice tables of native
hardwoods. All of them were covered with heavy
crocheted doilies.

"Your tables are so beautiful," I said. "Why do you
cover them?"

"The doilies make me feel less homesick," she said,
turning from the window. "We used to have them in our
living room at home. My grandmother crocheted them."
She was silent again, watching the horizon from a chair
into which she had sunk wearily.

I remembered a returning missionary on the ship who had been nursing a dying geranium. She had brought it to my botanist husband for a diagnosis, and I asked her why she carried a sick geranium to a land where orchids hung out of the trees.

"It grew above our kitchen sink," she had said, and there were tears in her eyes. "Wait until you have been out *there* a while."

The missionary had said *there* as though our destination were too horrible to call by name. I remembered that when Bob and I packed, we had put an ear of red Indian corn from our garden in my steamer trunk.

"Tell me about your work," I had said, hoping to distract her and learn something at the same time. "What sort of place do you live in? What do you eat? What do you do for fun?"

"*Fun!*" Very amazed. "I'm not out there for fun."

"Of course. Your station is in the interior, isn't it? Life must be pretty difficult." I felt I had said something in bad taste.

"It isn't any one thing that gets you," she said. "It's all the little things. Jiggers, for instance, and bouts of fever, and having to boil your drinking water, and getting skin diseases that itch, and tropical ulcers that won't heal." She showed me huge round scars on her legs.

"What are jiggers?" I thought I might as well hear all the worst now that we had started.

"They're little animals that lay eggs in your skin, usually on your feet. After a few days you feel a terrible itching and see a little pinpoint of black. Then it's time to lift out the egg sack. It has to come out whole. If you break it, the eggs scatter in the tissues and hatch. Then you're in for trouble. Natives lose their toes that way."

"How big is this egg-sack?" My feet felt itchy.

"Oh, about the size of a June pea. After you get it out you have to pour the hole full of iodine. That's the worst thing about it. Sometimes they are under the nail, and then it's more difficult. You must never step on the bare floor."

"I won't!" I said emphatically.

"It's when all these little things pile up on you that you get homesick," she said. "It isn't any big, dramatic danger like a charging elephant that takes bravery; it's courage for little things. And then is when you would not trade one geranium from home for all the orchids in Africa."

"I guess life in Africa is pretty rugged," I said feebly.

"You have to put your trust in God," she said. "It's time for our group to have prayers now." She sighed as she walked heavily away.

"You have to have either God or Bols gin to keep from going crazy," said an old Coaster in the next deck chair who had overheard the conversation. "I'll take liquor. Will you come along to the bar?"

Doilies, Bols gin, red geraniums, and Indian corn! I saw that I would have to exterminate nostalgia and lethargy, to fight them the way one fought cockroaches. I would have to sift them out of my thinking the way Sammi sifted bugs out of the flour. *Why couldn't nostalgia be for the beautiful rather than for the familiar?*

"Six more months and we get out of this lousy place," my hostess was saying. I came back to the living room with a start.

"You won't be coming back here if you dislike it so much, I suppose?"

"Oh, sure. We'll come back. It's funny, when you get home you forget all about the things you complain about out here. We hate carrying our own packages and making our own beds and scrubbing the bathtub. Last time I was home, I could hardly wait to get back."

"Maybe we'll be going before we think if the rumors about an invasion of French Senegalese come true."

"Oh, I doubt it," she said. "This place lives on rumors. I don't believe all the talk about those air bases in French Guinea and that business about the French putting a railroad down across the Sahara. People get bored with nothing to talk about besides rubber, so they make up rumors."

After lunch Bob and I started out to hunt coffee and other food. There were two ways to go; toward the coast where the Americo-Liberians had so-called "farms," or toward Salala, the village at the end of the motor road leading toward the interior. We asked Johnny's advice.

"Well, Missy, I can't say. When a native man makes farm he means he plants rice. We-part can't eat eggs only for medicine. Papaya and pineapple and oranges are small-boy chop. Sometimes the Liberian people can use such things. Better we try the Liberians. For myself, I like to find some stoffi."

"What is stoffi?"

"Stoffi is stoffi, Missy."

"Is that a Bassau word?"

"Missy, you can't hear [understand] English?"

"Explain my language, then," I said tartly.

He disappeared and came back with a smelly wooden box.

"I think you can put your eye on the name your ear cannot hear," he said.

The box was labeled "Stockfish."

"Oh! Stockfish."

"That's what I said, Missy. Stoffi!"

"Tell me, Johnny, where did you learn English?"

"Well, Missy, so soon I talk Bassau, my pa took me and we walk by land ti' we come Monrovia. My pa give me to one government man. That Liberian talk fine law-yer-English. So I learn lawyer-English. Plenty Bassau men carry boy-pickin to Monrovia so they learn English and grow up to do white-clothes work. Poor Boy learn English same-way. But Sammi! Sammi learn on the plantation. He learn cook-work and talk by being small-boy in a kitchen. Sammi do' talk proper and he do' take proper care for fine clothes. Bush remain in Sammi.

"And now, Missy, you can allow me to ride to the gate with you and I get down and look for my small stoffi?"

"Stockfish," I said firmly.

"Yes, Missy, that is the one I said. Stoffi."

Toward the coast, then! We turned off the main Monrovia road, and stopped at numerous Americo-Liberian places. Instead of building their houses of mud as the native tribesmen do, they use corrugated iron or wood. The floors are loose planks with large cracks between them. Most of the houses start out as huge frames with

wide verandas, but many of them are never fully en-
closed with walls. The floor of the veranda may rot away
before a roof is added. Scrollwork around the eaves is
much in vogue. The ornate decoration is pathetic grandeur on the desolate shells.

At one of the Liberian houses we stopped and met the family. The man was tall and stooped. He wore a pair of black woolen trousers much too large for him. They were green with age in the seams and were held up on his gaunt frame with a pair of new suspenders. His shirt was white, striped with purple, the kind made for detachable collars, but there was no collar around his wrinkled neck. The hand which he offered us in greeting was long and loose-jointed and protruded a surprising distance from the too short sleeves. In his other hand was a roach-eaten dictionary.

The Liberian's stocky wife radiated hospitality. She brought chairs of a mail-order variety from which the blistered veneer was peeling, and placed them on the veranda for us. When I sat on mine the loose plank under it tilted and I regained my equilibrium with an awkward jostle to a more secure board.

"So sorry, Madame," the Liberian said. "We agrarians have so little time to devote to improving our own domiciles."

Mrs. Liberian brought out a wooden tray with four dirty tumblers and a bottle of dusty-purple beverage. Her cotton dress was made in the typical Liberian style, very tight across breasts and buttocks and full at the waist where it was held into many gathers by a tight, narrow belt.

"Plum beer," she said. "We make it ourselves."

I looked at Bob for a cue. We had been warned many times about the danger of dysentery from drinking palm wine. But how to refuse graciously? There was probably not enough alcohol in it to make it safe.

"Thank you so much," my husband said, "but I never drink when I am driving a car. Could we take the bottle with us and save it until we get home to enjoy?"

"Most certainly," he said. "Here, Charity, wrap this bottle and give it to the servant in the motorcar."

Charity was a leggy little girl of light color, playing in the yard with a chipped blond doll. She wrapped the bottle in a banana leaf, stood under the clump of bananas, and called, "Here, boy! Come yah!" in an authoritative voice.

Poor Boy climbed slowly out of the pickup at her command and went to take the bottle. Charity was then sent to see whether the chickens had laid any eggs in the cassava patch.

A few hunks of dried rubber lay on the end of the piazza. The Liberian explained it.

"You see," he said, "it is necessary for me to augment my meager salary as a minister of the gospel, so I made elaborate plans to turn my holdings here into a plantation. I first tried coffee but we are at the mercy of the world market. It was not profitable, so I let my coffee trees go to bush."

He indicated the vine-knotted vegetation at the right of the piazza.

"Do you have coffee for sale?" I interrupted. "We would like to buy a hundred pounds."

"No, madam, I regret that I did not get around to harvest any of the beans this season. After the coffee failed, I decided to grow rubber. However, my project was inhibited by the unavailability of native labor, and I was forced to allow the seedlings to remain in yonder nursery. The lethargy of the indigenous population is beyond comprehension. My children tap the trees, and we allow the latex to run down the trunks for lack of suitable receptacles in which to catch it. When it is dry, the children collect it and we obtain a meager honorarium from it. The price of ground scrap is very low, however. It has been necessary to turn to making cane juice in order for me to support my family. *Nitor in adversum!*"

He looked sideways at us to see if we had been impressed by the Latin phrase.

"Yes," he went on in a pulpit voice, "I struggle against adverse circumstances. But the acid of bitterness has not etched my soul, glory be to God, whose humble servant I am. I am trained in the profession of law, but it is better for me to labor here among the wayward souls in straitened circumstances than to try to compete with the colleagues in my profession in Monrovia."

Poor Boy had been squinting at the sun through four eggs which Charity brought him while we heard about the Liberian's tribulations. The Liberian turned on him furiously.

"What do you mean by looking at the sun through my eggs, *bush boy!* You are not making purchases from a native!"

"Yes, sir!" Poor Boy answered, and I saw the blue color of his tribal mark deepen in a flush.

"Excuse me, sir and madam." The Liberian bowed to us. "These natives are entirely lacking in the finer precepts of courtesy."

Bob, eager to change the subject, indicated an exotic

pom-pom of white flower growing on a high shrub. "What is that plant?" he asked.

"It's peach," the Liberian said.

"But it isn't what we call peach at home."

"Well," he explained, "the fruit looks a little like peaches in the United States. When the first colonists came over here, they were so homesick they just called it that."

I noticed that the Liberian limped as he walked out to the car with us.

"I have tropical ulcers and they refuse to heal," he said. He pulled up the dirty trouser leg and a mesh of long underwear full of holes and showed us the angry-looking, festering sores. Tied around the calf of his leg was a leather pouch.

"This," he said, indicating the pouch, "is a charm that one of the native doctors made for me, but it does not prove effective."

"What is in it?" I asked.

"That is a secret of African science," he said. The medicine man asked me to bring him a young cockerel, and sheep dung, but of course he added curative herbs to the chicken blood and dung. Perhaps if you come this way again, you could bring me some medicine from the Firestone hospital? Meanwhile, I will save eggs for you from our fowls and watch for fresh vegetables and fruits for you."

"Aren't you afraid you will get infection from that leather bag next to those running sores?" I said. What I thought was, How is it that you who think you are so superior to the natives would go to a medicine man for treatment?

"Oh, no," he said. "One never acquires infection from the ministrations of a country doctor. Those fellows are really masters of African science, you know. They make medicine against infection. The Buzies have especially strong medicine. I always have medicine made for luck by one of them. But I have incurred the displeasure of a Mano man and I fear he has made stronger medicine for evil and that my Buzi luck medicine cannot stand up against it. Of late the tides of Fortune have run against me. The Manos have very strong medicine for evil."

We discussed the Liberian as we drove home. A minister selling the demoralizing cane juice to the natives! A man who believed that the tide of Fortune was against him because he was too lazy to work his farm! High-powered English and Latin phrases tossed off in a grand manner from a porch with rotten boards!

The way in which the Liberians dubbed that wild flower a "peach" reminded me of my conversation with my neighbor and I told my husband about the crocheted doilies, and how they in turn had reminded me of the missionary with the geranium and the old Coaster with his fondness for Bols gin.

"What's the matter with this country?" I said. "Everyone, including the missionaries and the drunks and the Liberians and the plantation people, seems to have nostalgia eating his heart out. Only the natives, as far as I can see, are free from it, and they *belong* here. Maybe the rest of us don't!"

Our discussion ended abruptly when the pickup went through a termite-riddled bridge. While Poor Boy cut reinforcements with his long knife, I went into the jungle to see if there might be some interesting plants to collect. I forgot about the saw grass that cut my shoes and arms and legs when I saw a patch of lush purple fungi, the color and shape of morning-glories.

"Morning-glory fungus!" I said, as I presented one to my perspiring husband. He looked at me queerly.

"Are you a victim, too?" he asked.

"Victim of what?"

"Your calling that thing in your hand 'morning-glory fungus' is just like the Liberians calling that bush shrub a 'peach.' You're remembering the morning-glories that grow on the gray stone wall at home. We'll look up the *name* of this! Peaches and doilies . . . " He looked grim.

We collected many interesting plants as we drove on home, but we found neither eggs nor coffee for sale.

Poor Boy carried all the plant specimens into the house and put them in the bathtub with cold water to keep them fresh until Bob could start identifying them.

"Well, Poor Boy," I said, "we didn't get much chop, did we?"

"No, Missy," he said, "but we catch plenty boss-part flowers and *four spoiled eggs!*"

"Let's go hunting," I said. "Maybe we shall see some wild guinea."

I wanted to hunt in order to tramp off a gnawing restlessness that had beset me that morning, and been growing all day. Somehow there must be a way to find deep beauty and song in daily living in this country. It was not a ready-made happiness; it had to be discovered. For myself and my household I would have to find the way to make a new song in a strange land.

I left Bob in a big armchair surrounded by plant specimens and botany books and plant keys. I noticed that he was starting with the purple fungus.

After Poor Boy and I had hunted for some time without seeing anything at which to shoot, we climbed to the top of Club House Hill where I could watch the sunset.

If Michelangelo had modeled with clouds instead of carving in stone, he might have sculptured the cloud figure I saw in the sky. He would have called it *Jehovah!* There was blue shadow between the cylindrical thighs, and into that shadowy blue valley a veil of silver beard cascaded like a waterfall. The fists were great masses that rested on the knees and they were clenched, not in anger but because, just at that moment, there was nothing to create. I could not see His face; it was turned into the sky as though He were deciding whether or not to call down a little rain.

He turned then, as a breath of wind rotated the alabaster throne, and the trailing cloud robes that flowed from His figure down to the horizon changed from blues and golds into purples and red-violet and crimson.

"What do you say this time, Missy?" asked Poor Boy, who was leaning against the stump where I was sitting. He meant what did I think about the sunset.

"I think," I said, "that I have seen God."

"Missy, I want to ask you something."

"What something, Poor Boy?"

"When a white person sees God, has God got a white face?"

"I did not see His face, Poor Boy. I would fear to look on the face of God. But I will tell you what I think."

"What's the one you are thinking, Missy?"

"I think that the side of God's face that is to the sun will be bright, and the side that is toward the night will be dark, so that no one can say that the face of God is any color at all."

Poor Boy was quiet a long time. Finally he said, "Missy, tonight in the camp I will tell the people the thing you tell me just now. It can make all we glad."

We had neither meat nor eggs to eat with our rice that night, and fortunately, no guests. We did have a long talk over our "dry rice" (the term by which the natives describe plain rice without meat or palm-oil "soup" to put over it). A peculiar desperate expression always comes over their faces when they say it. Dry rice is something to fill the belly, to be eaten without smacking of lips or rolling of eyes in ecstatic enjoyment.

There was something of dry-rice desperation in our conversation. We talked of all the glorious things we had hoped to accomplish, of how they had become as important to us as meat and palm oil to the natives' rice. We had been in the country two weeks and had not begun any of the projects we had outlined. The few plants my husband had collected had been ruined by cockroaches and mold. I had not done any carving because I could not carve without a work bench, and there were not any planks available. I had not modeled in clay because the

man who had agreed to bring me good clay had not returned. I had done two water colors, but the cockroaches
had eaten the paint from them during one night. I had
not been in the jungle because I had not been able to
borrow water canteens and because labor was scarce on
the plantation and I could not get carriers.

One of the most disconcerting things which had met
my attempts to learn native folkways and customs was the
answer which I had from them time after time, "No-o,
Missy. You can't know that one. It not your part to
know. *Bwaho!*"

There is nothing more negative than an African
"Bwaho." Behind a "no" in English or French there is
always lurking a possible "maybe," especially if it has
not been said emphatically. But behind even a mild and
courteous bwaho there is nothing but an insurmountable
wall. One may as well turn one's feet into other paths.

My plans were going the way of the Liberians' unfinished houses and vine-clotted plantations. And I recog-
nized that gnawing restless feeling; I was homesick!

"We'll make a list," Bob said. My husband has great
faith in the curative powers of list-making. They are the
first step in solving anything from the household budget
to a stubborn research problem. We made separate lists
and bravely headed them: THINGS TO ACCOMPLISH IN LI-
BERIA. When they were an impressive length, we both
felt a little better.

When the servants came to tell us their separate good
nights, as was their custom, Poor Boy said, "No mind for
the dry rice, Missy. Tomorrow we can see some good
thing. I go now for camp and tell my people the fine

thing you tell me on the hill this afternoon before the sun sleep."

"The natives are entirely lacking in the finer precepts. . . . " the Liberian had said.

"I think we must turn more and more to the natives, to supply us with song for our days," I said to Bob when the boys had gone.

"And for chop for our stomachs," he said. "We'll go toward Salala to market after this. Anyway, I have for today the name of that Liberian 'peach' and the purple fungus."

"And I have for today a sunset, and a little more understanding with a native boy," I said.

It was a good note on which to finish the evening. I thought I could bear to leave the ear of red Indian corn in the trunk a little longer!

CHAPTER FOUR

Teangalo Guana Days

AFTER our fruitless search for food among the Americo-Liberians, we tried our luck with the natives who live
in small villages between the plantation and the end of
the motor road leading toward the interior.

Big baskets for limes, the bamboo cages for chickens
and ducks, benzene tins for sweet potatoes, raffia rice bags
for eggs, empty whiskey bottles for palm oil, country
cloths for the boys to huddle beneath during the rains,
cigarette tins full of small coins — all these supplies for
the trip were noisily collected.

A last-minute drink against the thirst of the seventy-
mile trip! A last-minute shout to collect Poor Boy and
Isaac and Car Boy, the three converging from different
directions toward the pickup, speeding up their flying
black legs with the speeding of the motor, shouting lest
they be left behind! They land with a thud in the back
of the car, clutch their rain-battered old felt hats, and
shout, "Let go, Boss!" All this and we are off. Something
of the gusto of the occasion would be lost if we ever left
the house calmly and quietly.

We wind with the road through the rubber to the

boundary of the plantation where a pole bars our way. A native copes with the intricacy of the number on the car, records it, and allows us to pass. Helter-skelter mud huts line the road outside the gate; there is none of the enforced orderliness of the plantation. Africans as well as nature abhor a straight line! Mongrel dogs and scrawny chickens sun themselves in the dust of the road, and move reluctantly from the tracks. Cassava patches on either side of the road have replaced the parklike rows of rubber.

We get the sun in our eyes through the windshield. It reflects shimmering heat from the hood of the car. In the valley, before the steep hill to Kakata, the usual number of naked women are standing knee-deep in the creek, bathing and washing clothes. Slender trails of suds float

whitely in the stream and disappear beneath the uncertain plank bridge which we slow down to cross.

We turn to the right in Kakata, at the corner where the District Commissioner hears palavers in the big courthouse with the iron roof. The plank shutters are open and look through the window holes at intent rows of African profiles concentrated on the peculiar formalities that satisfy the natives' keen craving for justice.

Sometimes we stop at the post office to mail letters from the only "interior" post office in Liberia. The mud post office is also a bakery and a store. The shelves are bare except for a few bottles of ginger beer with bubbles boiling toward the top of the amber fluid. One calls for the postmistress, who appears from the rear of the house and disappears again to hunt for stamps.

Beautiful stamps! Birds and animals and air mail, though there is no air-mail service within Liberia. Stamps stuck on carefully with paste swabbed from an almost empty pot. Letters left on the unpainted counter will arrive in the States months later.

If we carry a letter to a friend in the interior, we will not stamp it; it will go *tatua* from the end of the road. We will give it to a Buzi man in Salala, who will send it to the next town. The chief in that town will send it with a runner to the next town. A tatua note will arrive anywhere in the interior promptly and safely.

North of Kakata the marketing begins. All three boys shout at the top of their lungs as we drive along, "Chicken, chicken-egg . . . paw-paw, pineapple . . . banana, cassava. . . . " It is a rhythmic, gusty song. The ex-

citement of the trip puts the boys in powerful voice. Poor Boy yells in Bassau, Isaac in Kpuesi, and Car Boy in whichever seems to need his support.

At the native villages the boys always find "goo' friends" to tell "How-do, yah?" who snap fingers and dash them sugar cane to suck noisily along the way, or pineapples to peel with huge knives and eat between stops with an extravagance of sweet juice lost on their chins.

"*Teangalo! Teangalo Guano?* [Do chicken-eggs leave your house today?]"

Sometimes it's "Aye, aye!" The boys drum on the roof of the cab, we slide to a stop, and chicken-eggs appear. Sometimes it is one egg, sometimes two, rarely, as many as eight, for which abundance the owner is dashed a ha'penny. Poor Boy encircles each egg with his fingers, holds it to his eye, and squints toward the sun. The natives cannot understand why we insist on "the new egg."

While the inspection is going on, the villagers crowd around the car, curious, grinning, friendly. They discuss the length of my hair, they look inside the cab to see my shoes, they point at my red fingernails.

Gradually we fill the raffia bag with small, dirty fowl eggs. A duck egg "can cost one cent past chicken eggs; it big, yah?" The road is grooved with ruts and full of puddles. Calling it a road is sheer euphemism. I hold the bag of eggs away from me, clutching it with both hands, hoping my body will absorb enough of the jar to save the thin shells. Why do the recipes of so many good things to eat require eggs?

We have come to know many of the natives along the way. One emaciated old man with a mighty crop of fuzzy hair wears a long, black silk dress. His name is Chief-Smith's-Brother. His dress fits him skimpily, and suffers severe strain at the seams when he leans forward purposefully from the hips and takes out in high gear after a flighty chicken he hopes to catch for our inspection.

Chief-Smith's-Brother is the owner of a Dominic rooster with a bright red comb. This bird is actually bright-eyed, aggressive-looking, and almost as large as an American rooster. Compared to the usual bleary-eyed, straggling man-chicken, this is indeed a paragon among cocks. We look at him covetously, and try to buy him. Nothing doing!

"That one," Brother tells us, "is the man-of-the-yard! If I sell that one, the woman-chicken can't lay egg again."

We can understand that Man-of-the-Yard is no doubt an inspiration to the sparsely feathered females of the compound; but we try, unsuccessfully, to convince Brother that roosters fertilize eggs but do not make hens lay. This is an old argument with which we have never convinced a native, so we drive on regretfully.

At the end of the road at the village of Salala, there are always carriers who have arrived from the interior with huge loads on their heads and backs. Rice and cola nuts and country cloth and chickens flow in endless procession down the divergent trails that lead to Mano country and French Guinea on the right, and to Buzi country and Sierre Leone on the left.

We get out of the car to stretch and talk to the villagers at Salala, and I look longingly down the foot trails that lead to the interior. Beyond is the real interior, almost unmapped, unexplored, pagan, mysterious! Someday, I will set my feet on these paths, someday I will see where they lead. . . . I can see only to the next hill; someday I will see the next, and the next. Someday I will cross the country to Ganta.

Baysah is a prosperous Buzi trader with a gold tooth that gleams in the sun when he grins his welcome.

"What thing you save for we today, Baysah?"

"I got country cloth, but not for money-part. American cloth, ah hah!"

American cloth is the ticket to Baysah's back room where there are country cloths and ground-pea, and small onions from the French side.

The pickup is piled high now, but a few natives hail us as we start home. One man from whom we buy an egg or two regularly usually has another one by the time we pass his hut again. I asked him once about this curious "one-more-again egg."

"Well, Ma," he explained, "when the motorcar pass, I look at all the woman-chicken. Sometime, one can have egg-look in the eye. Then I catch that one, and I force her until you come again."

"But the chicken, she can no agree for force," I argued.

"No-o, she no agree, so she give up the egg. You see?"

"I no need to see the sun through this one," Poor Boy grinned. "It new-o, like hell-o!"

"It new, too much," I said grimly. "Let go, yah."

No matter what time we leave home during the rainy season, "the clouds cry; rain catch we." Not much marketing is achieved in a deluge. The boys sit huddled damply under the blue-and-white-striped country cloth where three humps indicate the source of muffled and not very enthusiastic mutterings for chicken-egg.

After the sudden screening of the horizon by a blue-black wall of ominous cloud, there is sometimes to be seen against that screen the silhouette of a leafless tree, startlingly white and alone. The bleached cleanness of the skywarding trunk, and the intricate lace of the small branches that cap it, are so dramatic that for a moment the white tree and the indigo backdrop are all of the landscape, and all of the world. We descend the hill, losing sight of the tree, and I feel that for one rare moment I have looked on the inside of a dream, where the ecstasy of an unworldly white and perfect thing is felt against the velvet depths of sleep.

Sometimes, "the clouds fini cry, before the sun sleep." Then a "water-bow" arches across the sky. I look at the generous arc of its circle and find my spirits lifting toward the color and the curve of the bow. Sometimes I wonder how men would have fashioned it. Some would have pinched it up into a cramped Gothic arch and some would have used it to sky-write their names. I am increasingly glad for the beauty of a circle.

Dusk is quickly consummated. There are only a few moments when the mimosa, no longer green, but black now, is seen as lacy filigree against a lighter sky. Then all the world is dark save for the fires in the villages where ebony figures are silhouetted against red glow in a world that is enormously big with its blackness. Sometimes, a pair of eyes catch fire in the path of the headlights and an animal slinks away in the bush. One says, without really meaning it, "I should have brought a gun. Someone got a leopard here last week." The cab is a little island of life in mysterious big blackness, and the talk turns dreamy and reminiscent. The boys in the back nod with the motion of the cab, asleep, with their backs against the cab, their heads lolling forward.

Finally, ahead there are the yellow lights of home. Steaming food and fragrant coffee . . . wonder who will

be there for chop . . . greetings . . . quick change to dinner clothes . . . music . . . good food . . . unhurried talk
. . . drowsy good nights. The wind is rustling the travelers' palm, drums are throbbing in the camp, and
crickets talk in the yard.

CHAPTER FIVE

Ju-Ju Before Dinner

Our hunting had been poor for a week. The last quarter of antelope was finished. The Salala route was overworked and the last Wednesday trip had yielded little food. As usual there would be people in for evening chop. I decided to walk to the Jacobtown market eight miles distant from the road.

Jacobtown market is smelled and heard long before it is seen. The sound is a merged chatter, shrill and rapid. The smell is a blend of smoked elephant hide, rancid palm oil, village goats, and human perspiration.

Women with loads of rice and cassava on their heads and babies on their backs converged into the main path from smaller trails all along the way. They wore their best clothes and jewelry. There was a throb of excitement and expectation in the air. Some of them had walked since early morning.

A large dugout carried passengers across the river. The fare is one cent in dry time, two cents in the rainy time. People crowd into the canoe with their loads of produce until the waterline is dangerously near the top. A dozen people were in the canoe ahead of me. It sank lower into the water. Only the week before a canoe had capsized, drowning three persons.

"Tell the boatman," I instructed Poor Boy, "that the load is sufficient. Let the remaining people wait and I dash him sixpence."

The boatman agreed and I tossed him a coin. However, natives continued to jump into the boat which settled still deeper.

"Bwaho! Bwaho!" I complained, "How is it that I dash the man but he allows more people to get into the canoe?"

"The boatman says," interpreted Poor Boy, "he agrees the boat is full, but he can no stop the people from jumping inside. All he can do is leave soon."

"Help him shove off, then!"

Natives were standing knee-deep in water trying to force their way into the boat as we rowed away. The boat rocked dangerously as people tried to settle their head loads in the bottom.

When we were finally across, an old woman took my hand and brushed her palms lightly as a butterfly across mine, and jabbered something in Kpuesi.

"The old woman say," Poor Boy told me, "that God bless the canoe because white woman sit there, else we all sleep soon in the crocodile's belly."

"Never mind. You run ahead, look everywhere for meat. Goat, sheep, chicken, duck, antelope . . . anything we can chop."

Natives with head loads of rice and cassava rushed ahead of me to spread the news that a white woman was coming to the market. A great shout went up from the colorful mob as I appeared. The chief's bell ringer set up a great clatter with two old brass bells and two soldiers cleared a path through the crowd through which the chief walked to greet me. He wore the usual blue-and-white-striped country cloth and a large brimmed felt hat. We snapped fingers. A great howl of acclaim went up from the crowd. We walked side by side to a mound of earth where soldiers set a chair for me and another for the chief. A soldier blew a whistle and the crowd sat in its tracks, silent and attentive. The chief rose then and made a long speech, waving an elephant tail as he gestured. Part of the speech, of which I could not understand a word, seemed to concern me. The elephant tail was waved toward me and the crowd nodded and stared. A soldier collected two cents from each seller, and another wave of the elephant tail indicated that bargaining could begin. The crowd shouted and surged. Many of them crowded around me looking at my red fingernails and pointing at my hair.

The chief sent for his interpreter.

"Ma, the people like to know do the fingers on the feet grow red same way like hands."

I obliged by taking off my shoes and socks. The red toenails brought a shout that doubled the mob which pressed around me. They ran their fingers over the lacquered surfaces of the nails on my great toes.

"Fine," they said, "Fine too much." One old lady looked over the shoulders of the mob and screamed while the others laughed. "She thinks it's blood," they told me and laughed more.

"Excuse, please," I said to the chief when I finally had my shoes on again. "I come to buy."

"The chief say," said the interpreter, "what thing Ma like to buy?"

"I need meat past all chop," I said. "But also I like to buy chicken-egg, and plenty banana and pineapple."

The chief spoke to the soldier who brought a clay pot full of soup in which swam what looked to me like a child's hand. There were the long nails on fingers still attached.

"What is it?" I said, feeling a little sick.

"Fine, fine baboon soup, Ma. You like to buy that

one? All the people want some, but the chief say the white ma must have first part."

"Tell the chief I say thank you plenty, yah, but I no fit to chop the fine soup. The baboon, it taboo for my part."

An odor that almost suffocated me passed under my nose with some gray baconlike slabs of smoked meat.

"Elephant hide from Gbebie, Ma. It can make strong soup."

"I like antelope meat," I said. "Ask the chief for the antelope part. Plenty people come for my house to chop, and no meat stay there this time. You tell the chief he find the antelope for me, he can see fine dash."

"No antelope today, Ma. Only the baboon soup, the elephant hide, the big snake, and rats. No antelope. The rats, he fine. Ma can't like the rat part?"

"No," I said. "I can't see my-part chop here this time. Better we go for home. The way be far."

The walk home from the market was beautiful. The single-file procession of native women going up the hill ahead of me with huge loads of rice and cassava root and sweet potatoes on their heads was a study in ebony against the green jungle that rose like the steep sides of a canyon on either side of the narrow trail. Wild cannas bloomed crimson among the pineapples which had sprung up from discarded tops thrown on the ground on former market days. The evening light was dim with a reddish cast. The shadows under the huge trees were purplish pockets of mystery. The loud market-chatter was stilled. We walked purposefully and silently, the women to their scattered villages; I to my house. What would I have for dinner?

"*Allez*, Ma! *Allez!* The sun, he sleep soon-o. Dark can catch we." Sahba Jo, my yard boy, walking behind me with a crate of sweet potatoes on his head, wanted me to hurry. Poor-Boy-No-Friend Washman walked behind him with a hundred pounds of rice in a raffia bag on his head. Paper Bag followed with a load of miscellany.

I turned out to pass the woman ahead of me who was trying to retie the baby on her back without removing from her head a bamboo crate containing two chickens. The boys muttered an apology in the Kpuesi language as we passed.

"Ma, it is necessary to excuse when one person pass other person on path," Poor Boy explained. "Better Ma learn the excuse. Excuse in English can't be excuse, proper. Excuse in English be so-so words from the mouth; excuse in Kpuesi be talk from the heart."

I ignored the devastating comment.

"Some other time, I learn the Kpuesi, Poor Boy. Make we go, yah, just now!" We passed others on the trail.

"Ma, how many person can wait for chop, sat down at bungalow?" Sahba Jo asked the question I had been pondering myself. There was no way of telling how many guests there would be for dinner in this hotelless country. We had bought only a few eggs, not sufficient for an omelet, even if we used them all. Paper Bag had squinted at the sun through the eggs as we bought them and announced several times, "Ma, small-boy chicken can leave these egg, soon-o."

What meat would we have for dinner, and how many people would be waiting to eat it? It would have to be those bleary-eyed half-dozen chickens we had been feeding good rice in the hope that eventually one of them would lay an egg.

Maybe tonight we would shoot an antelope. But first, there was the matter of dinner.

The light was brighter when we left the jungle shadows of the forest and crossed the river to the plantation. Sammi met me on the path a half mile from home, looking disconsolate.

"You bring meat from the market, Missy? I do' know what to cook for chop. Plenty people come, sit down. I heat plenty, plenty ground-pea. All the people eat, eat, ti' Hungry can't catch people soon-time, but I do' know what to cook for the time Hungry do come."

"What people come for chop, Sammi?"

"Well, Missy, I can't say. Four be missionary from interior. Two strange men that can't be missionary. Three goo' friends from plantation, self. Two more again strange man that no talk English, sometime their-part talk sound French. Altogether eleven people make self Missy's stranger. Missy and Massio make altogether thirteen people for table."

"How you know the two strange men that talk English no be missionary part?"

"Missy, I can *smell* missionary part."

"Nonsense, Sammi. Missionaries smell like anyone else, only no alcohol."

"Missy, you no hear me good. We-part no smell with the nose; we-part smell with the heart."

"The word, Sammi, is *intuition*."

"Thank you, Missy. I smell intuition. Now, what for chop?"

"You run, one time, kill all the chicken that live for chicken-bungalow. I think six chicken can stay there."

"But the Massio? He can vex for chicken die? Massio say the chicken must lay chicken-egg."

"Massio has got to eat. You run, do the one I tell you."

"Yeah, Missy. I go before. But first, what place I can see cane juice?"

"Cane juice? You tell me you do' drink cane juice. Mu [go]! Get gone! I vex."

"Missy, I tell you true. The cane juice no be my-part. Is necessary the chicken be drunk to die-o. Chicken no drunk, meat strong-o, knife can't cut."

"In my country, we no make chicken drunk to die."

"But Missy, you do' know Liberian-part chicken!"

"O.K. You go tell Watchman give you one cup cane juice. Soon-morning time, I pay him."

"But Missy, one cup not sufficient."

"Do you mean to tell me that six chicken can drink past one cup cane juice?"

"No, Missy. It not all chicken part."

"One cup!" I said firmly. "No time to palaver. Now you run, make stove hell-o hot, kill the chicken."

Thirteen people! Six chickens to get intoxicated before they could be killed. Dark falling fast! Well, the guests had been eating plenty peanuts, Sammi had said.

When I entered the living room, I found my guests, tall glasses in hand, gathered in front of the French windows, regarding a scene on the lawn. Sammi was holding open a chicken's mouth and Johnny was pouring something down its gullet from an old tin can. The fowl fluttered loose and was snatched by the tail. More liquid was forced down her throat. After a few seconds the boys released her. She looked dazed. She lifted a foot experimentally and tried to take a step. She fell flat on her beak. . . . Uproarious shouts. A drum under our house tuned up with experimental thuds while the chicken's feet were being tied with a piece of vine, and Sammi went for his swordlike Bassau knife, and a snort from the tin can. The drum found its rhythm, a slow emphatic repetition of thumps.

Sammi knelt in front of the chicken and bowed his forehead to the ground. His elevated rear, turned toward the house, was decorated by sparse remnants of trouser. A felled seam down the middle of the back still held but large circles of the material on either side had worn away from having been sat upon, so that one saw more Sammi than trouser. The other servants formed a circle around Sammi and the chicken.

Sammi rose, retired to the edge of the circle, advanced to the chicken again, and sat down on the grass with his knees against his chin and his arms quietly entwined around himself in the position of a fetus. Slowly he lifted his head and listened as the drum rolled. Then he stuck his neck out, experimentally, slowly unfolded legs and arms, rose to his feet shakily, shook his body as though discovering for the first time how it worked, smoothed his bare mahogany skin, and began to dance with his feet only, holding his body rigid. Gradually, he let the movement flow upward through his body until every rippling muscle was flowing with the accelerated beating of the drum.

The entire circle danced, then, twisting, turning, yelling, leaping, but none as violently as Sammi. The drum played faster and faster, Sammi leaped higher and higher. His eyes rolled. His teeth flashed as he jerked his head upward from his chest on the heavy beat of the drum pattern. His knife flashed and flourished. Foam showed on his lips. With one final yell which sent ice running down my hair roots, Sammi leaped high and plunged the knife downward to the chicken's heart. He fell and lay motionless on the ground beside the chicken. The pageant of life, from birth to death by blood lust, was finished.

Five to go, I thought. I wonder if I couldn't go down quietly and chop their heads off with an axe.

Johnny waited on the steps. "Missy," he said, "the bush is strong in Sammi. When he learn to dance so, *it was not chicken* he killed."

Under the house I found Animal Boy. "Where the other chicken?" I asked.

"Ma, I got to tell you something." Animal Boy was frightened.

"Tell me some other time. I want the remainder of the chicken, just now."

"Ma, it be chicken-part palaver I got to talk."

"Hurry."

"Ma, last night driver ants come to chicken-bungalow. One chicken sit for the tree. That one die by Sammi just now. But the part that live for the house, all die. This morning, only small bone and plenty feather remain."

"How you can't tell me, soon-morning time?"

"Ma, I fear too much."

"How you can't hear the chicken cry in the night when the driver come?"

"Ma, I no stay under the house last night. I sleep for the camp. Yesterday-time, I buy me new woman. Oh, Ma, she hellova fine, my new woman!" He smiled ecstatically in recollection.

I was not very hungry as I climbed the back stairs to the kitchen. Sammi still lay motionless on the grass, the bloody knife beside him. The chicken was gone. Probably the boys were cleaning it in the servants' kitchen. Thirteen people, one chicken!

"Johnny, here keys for the chop cupboard. Open some Spam again, yah?"

"Yeah, Missy!"

CHAPTER SIX

Drumbeats of Hunger

Tɪᴍᴇ ꜰʟᴏᴡs in a hunger rhythm in a land where rice is every native's deepest concern. Years are counted by rice-plantings, seasons by the empty-time when the rice kitchens are bare and the full-time of harvest. Weeks are punctuated by market day; villages are named for the day on which their markets are held. On the plantation where the natives are cut off from the tribal supply, rice issue is the big event of the week.

"What day do all we take rice from your hand?" asked Sammi Cook, as soon as we had agreed on the important matter of salary, one shilling twopence a day.

"How about Mondays?" I said, thinking that Monday would be a good day to get squared away for the week.

"Bwaho, Missy! Monday can be a bad day for we to see rice."

"Why you can no agree for Monday?"

"Well, Missy, you see, Monday be the day for the Goatown market. Goa means 'Monday' in English. Plenty people pass this side for go market at Goatown on Goa day. Any Bassau man can sit down on me for chop. If rice stay for my house *it is necessary I give*. It is our law.

Suppose no rice stay here? Then I tell all them 'I sorry too much. Hungry live here. I can no see chop for your-part.' Then they go some other place, sit down on some other Bassau boy."

"What day, then?"

"The day after Goatown market can be a good day. Then all the rice can live for my belly before Goa day come again."

When Monday came, I saw what Sammi meant about people coming to sit down. All the space under the house was filled by ten o'clock, although market did not start until two and was only ten miles away. The women wore their best wrap-around *lappas* and a strange assort-ment of jewelry, including strings of safety pins. Their headcloths were wound into perky turbans flattened on top by the baskets of produce they carried. They bor-

rowed hunks of glowing charcoal from Poor Boy to light their clay pipes until they had exhausted the slender ironing supply.

I went under the house to try to buy some of the things they were carrying to sell. A first-chance market of my own!

"Bwaho, Missy. Bwaho!" one of the women said when I tried to buy some eggs.

"Ask the woman why she no agree to sell the eggs, Poor Boy."

"She say, Missy, that suppose she sell the egg to you, she have nothing remain to sell in the market."

"But," I argued, "if she carries the eggs to sell, what matter that I buy them before she reach Goa?"

"Missy, if a woman carry nothing for market, she cannot talk to plenty people. All the people, they go find the person with cargo to sell, and make bargain-talk. It be woman-part to like plenty talk."

The eggs went to Goatown along with the noisy crowd under the kitchen. I sent Sammi along with them to see what he could buy for me. When he came back late that night he had some withered snap beans, some bruised-looking eggplants, and a dozen eggs.

"The eggs be the same ones you try to buy from the woman this morning," he said. "I dash her small, and she save them for me. But they stay for the woman's hand till market finish. When all the boys from white man's house try to buy the egg, she have fine time, she talk plenty."

"You do fine-o, Sammi. *Gnahsuoh* [Thank you]!"

"Yeah, Missy, but the dash-part I give the woman, it be sweet soap you dash me yesterday." He looked sad.

"All right, tomorrow-time when I give rice, you can see more-again soap. In the United States we call the one you do a 'racket.' "

He looked puzzled. "But, Missio, I am thinking a racket be the thing we can no do under the house when it is the time the Massio like to sleep or he vex like hell-o."

"That's another meaning, Sammi. English is a very hard language."

"Yes," he said. "Too bad too much that English can't be easy like Bassau."

Sammi reminded me at breakfast next morning that it was the day after Goa.

"Of course," I said. "That is why we have eggs for breakfast."

"That is not the meaning of today to me-o, Missy."

"What is the meaning?"

"Missy, yesterday, I never take chop. I die for hungry. Today we take rice!"

"Go then, call all the boys to bring something to catch their-part rice."

I unlocked the chop cupboard and dipped cup after cup out of the bulging burlap bag. A cup is either an empty number 2 tin can or a "government cup" which looks larger but isn't, because "the bottom of the cup can't live for the bottom." I used a "salmon cup," the bottom of which Sammi had carefully pounded into convexity so it would hold a few more grains.

"The person with good ways puts all on top the cup

that can stay there," Sammi informed me. I heaped each cup. Each cup held a pound, and a pound was needed for each day of the week for each boy. Seven cups for Johnny, seven cups for Buno, seven cups for Poor Boy . . .

"Missy, I got woman," Poor Boy reminded me.

Seven cups for Poor Boy's woman.

"What about Monday-ca, Missy? Monday-man eats rice past me."

Rice was very short on the plantation. All the loads coming down country on men's heads had to run the gauntlet of the Liberian officials who sat in the larger villages. We had been asked to issue no more to a family than enough for a man and his wife. Without rice, the labor would go back to their tribes, and without labor, the rubber could not be produced.

"I am not allowed to issue rice for the pickin, Poor Boy, but let your woman bring Monday-ca to me and he can earn his rice."

"That small-boy can no walk, Missy. How he can earn rice?"

"He can sit for me and I will draw his photo."

Seven cups for Sammi, seven cups for Depumba, his woman.

"But Missy," Sammi objected. "I got two mammas."

"Sammi," I said, "already, I tell you that you cannot keep two mammas under my house at the same time. I don't care how many mammas you buy. I don't care if you have women past a paramount chief. But this one you must hear good: only one mamma can stay here at one time! Two mammas make palaver. When I want to sleep they put pepper in each other's eyes. When our good friends come and we want to talk softly-softly, two mammas chase each other with knives and scream like Kru women."

"Missy, no Bassau woman can make big-mouth like a Kru woman." I had touched a sore point of tribal pride.

"That, Sammi, is not the one we are talking."

"Well, Missy, I do' know how I can manage. My young mamma can no walk by land to Bassau because pickin can leave her soon. My young mamma is lazy. It is a big mistake to buy a young mamma. She refuse to cook my chop, she refuse to set my fish trap, she refuse to go for market to buy my small-small something. All these

things my old mamma do for me. So the young one cannot go, and the old one I have much need for. So, how
can I manage?"

"How soon can pickin leave the young mamma?"

"Well, Missy, we do' know that one, but she say it can
be soon-time." That it wouldn't be long was obvious
even to me.

"All right," I said. "She can stay until the pickin be
born. After that, you must send one of them to your
people. But I can give you rice for one only. Better you
send one of the small boys to Bassau to bring rice for
your plenty people. Boy-part rice fini. Now where the
calabash for the animal rice?"

The boys exchanged disgusted glances. The deplor-
able waste of *feeding* chickens! And that Bwi-u, the small
dog, getting rice as though he were a person! And Small
Meat, the zebra antelope! All the animals together ate as
much as one boy.

"Now you have each your-part rice, and Buno has the
rice to cook for the animals. Mu now, yah?"

The calabashes of rust-gold grain were lifted to the
boys' heads. They made a happy procession down the
back stairs. I had expected them to start cooking it at
once, but there was no mortar-thump in the servants'
kitchen.

"How is it that you don't cook?" I asked Johnny, who
was polishing the silver. "You told me that you did not
eat all day yesterday."

"Missy, when we say we do not eat, we mean that we
never take rice. We take small cassava, small sweet
potato, to hold we together. After a boy eats rice it is

necessary for him to sleep, and *sleep does not make the silver shine.*"

That evening after tea we went to the window and watched the rice being beaten in the mortars. Sammi's old mamma beat his rice without losing an ember of glowing charcoal off the top of her pipe. Poor Boy's mamma beat his rice without untying little Monday-ca from her back. His little head snapped with each plunge of the pole. Johnnie and Buno had to beat their own rice. Black arms raised high, ribs bowed tightly against the skin, feet rose on tiptoe for a moment and then the pestles were plunged into the mortars with force. They all beat with the same rhythm and sang an exuberant song, a tantalizing prelude to the feast. There remained only the threshing of the rice in fanners [panniers], up-ward-encircling swings and sideward movements, to rid the rice of waste and then the few minutes when it would bubble thickly in iron pots over blackened fire rocks.

As soon as our dinner had been served Johnny and Sammi ran down the back stairs. A dozen dark shadows hunched around a big enamel pan. Buttocks sought the earth, knees were cupped in armpits, bodies rocked on splayed feet in a flow of eagerness. Elbows swung out and fingers curled rice into balls, greasy with palm oil. Heads were thrown back and the missiles, bluish green with oil, were consumed with much rolling of eyes and sucking of lips. Fingers and chins became slick with palm oil and cast fleeting edges of green light into the growing shadows.

The movement of arms and the curling of fingers be-came intermittent as the rice diminished. The smacking of lips became articulate sounds of content. Half a week's supply of rice had been eaten in one sitting. In a few days the throbbing of empty stomachs would replace the throbbing of pestles against the mortars, eager move- ments would slow and footsteps would linger in their tracks. Hollow eyes and rigid faces would mirror the pulsing of empty stomachs, drumbeats of hunger.

When the servants came to tell us good night, Poor Boy brought Monday-ca along with him. He sat on Poor Boy's shoulder like a little monkey and held on to a fist- ful of his father's hair.

"Missy, the new boy come to ask what time he must begin his work."

"Tomorrow, soon-morning," I said. "Tell me, Poor Boy, how is it that you eat half your rice tonight, and hungry can catch you before rice day comes again?"

"Missy," he said, "I will tell you a story. One Buzi man tell it to me.

"Long, long time since, far to the north in the sand country [the Sahara] lived one big man named Hungry. His belly was hungry for rice and his heart was hungry for green trees. So he said to his people, 'Let me go to the land of the Buzis!' So he rolled up his sleeping mat, made small medicine for the journey, took bath in the waterside, and started on his way. The hot sand burned his feet, and the hot sun burned his head. When he died for tired, he say, 'Soon-time the big tree can make roof for my head.' And when he died for hungry, he say, 'Soon-time I come to the land of rice kitchens.' When he left the sand behind, he thought, After the strong grass of the flat Mandingo country, the way cannot be far.

"Soon the big tree came over his head, and his heart lie down for the green leaf, and the cold of the path caught his hot foot. Almost, he could hear the beat of the rice in the mortar, like drum-talk far away. So he say, 'I go, my heart lie down for the green leaf, but the rice be far from my belly.'

"So he passed for the Buzi town, and he say to the people, 'I make myself your stranger.' Then the people passed him plenty rice, and his belly still talk, and they bring him more again, and it still not sufficient. All

morning-time he eat, eat, all afternoon-time he eat, and
still he say, 'It not sufficient. Bring more.'

"But the people say, 'Our rice lack small to finish.
Small rice remain in the rice kitchen and empty-time
come soon.'

"Then old man Hungry threw a vex. And the people
say, 'This stranger have bad ways. Better the medicine
catch him.'

"In the night the medicine [poison] reach Hungry and
he die. Next day, plenty feast-day in the town. Old man
Hungry grow to be a long man as be the way with hungry people, so plenty meat stay for his bones. All the
people eat Hungry. But the meat can't lay for the Buzi
stomachs, and the people say, 'It must be that Hungry
curse we before he die.'

"And so all the people from that long time until now,
who help chop Hungry, and all their children for all
moon, feel always the curse of Hungry.

"And that, Missy, is the reason all black people stay
hungry for all time."

"But," I said, "how is it that hungry can catch you?
You be a Bassau boy, and yourself, you tell me plenty
times that even in old time, the Bassau people never
chop human meat. The Buzis, the Manos, the Gios, the
Kpuesi all say that their fathers know the leg of man is
sweet to chop, but the Bassau people do not know that
taste."

"It is true, Missy, that our people never chop person.
But I think that person can catch the curse of Hungry
the same way he catch the fever. *The curse lives for this*

country! We fight him all the time. First we have to cut
the big bush and the work is very hard. Then we plant
the rice and the rice birds come, so it necessary for the
small boys to stay always in the field with stones. Then
the bush cow come and spoil the field. Then we cut the
small part that remain, one stem, one stem, at a time

with a small knife, and plenty hurt catch the back. Then
we try to carry the rice and government people take from
we and if we refuse, they beat we with whips of bush-
cow hide. So when we see plenty rice, we make big
medicine against the curse for one night."

The little cooking fires had died to embers, and from
the servants' rooms came the deep breathing and snores
of those who were free for one night from the ancient
curse.

CHAPTER SEVEN

Poor Boy Looks at Our Culture

It was a damp morning when the flying termites emerged from the fog to beat off their wings against the screens. Poor Boy stood before the door of the laundry-sewing room which we had set up in one of the cells under the kitchen end of the house. He scuffed his bare toes thoughtfully in the six-inch-deep litter of wings, and fumbled with the lock.

"Here, Poor Boy! Let me do it," I said. The termites were fluttering down the neck of my dress and I could feel the wormlike bodies crawling on my skin.

Finally inside the whitewashed room, Poor Boy opened the windows, carried outdoors the odoriferous leopard and crocodile skins which were stored there, and dusted the sewing machine. He had a big ironing to do, and I had a stack of long-neglected mending. He bent over a charcoal grill he had made for heating the iron and puffed his cheeks into effective bellows. Ambrose, the omnipresent chimpanzee, rattled the screen and sat down on the ground to wait mournfully for the door to open. We had moved the ironing table inside from the laundry platform under the house to avoid Ambrose who liked to model freshly ironed clothing. I shook the termites out of my hair and sat down to work.

"The *Qui* [civilized people], Missy, are like the termites," Poor Boy said, as he watched the embers glow in the tin. "When they want something they go to it, fast and hard, though it break their wings. Black man can sit and wait like Ambrose, yonder, till the door open to him. Sometimes he waits until it is the pickin of his manchild that gets in the door."

"Yes," I said, "your people have a terrible patience. Sometimes I think this is a fine thing and sometimes it makes me fear. Your people should not always wait. Sometimes they could lift the latch. Not so?"

"True, Missy, but our people do not understand latch-palaver. That is white man's work. Our people do not know how to open the locks the white man makes. You know the way that old Town Chief Chimpanzee does with his lock. He takes a big rock and hits it with much noise, but it never open; he only spoil the lock. He do' know that small ticks one way, the proper ticks back the other way, make it open easy. When our people try to break the lock, it is in the way of Town Chief."

Poor Boy picked up an ancient copy of an American women's magazine which he used to keep the hot iron off the wooden table. He paged through it idly while I started to treadle an ancient affair which passed for a sewing machine. The only needles I had were made by a native blacksmith and they had a quirk of sewing neat little stitches for an inch or two and then galloping over the material without sewing at all, as though bored with the whole meticulous business. Poor Boy had a theory that castor oil would remedy anything — constipation, diarrhea, dandruff, or galloping sewing machines. When the serious threshing-machine sound of good sewing turned to a lighthearted dance, he would apply squirtings of oil which for the most part missed the oil holes and made sticky puddles on the material. He insisted that the oil had to have time to work, and after a brief spell, the machine usually sewed. I insisted that it was

obviously over-oiled and all it needed was a rest. These pauses gave us quiet for conversation, the only pleasant thing about the whole business.

Poor Boy looked up from his magazine while I waited for the oil to do the usual trick with the innards of the machine.

"I knew it, Missy! I knew it!" he shouted.

"You knew what?"

"American Neji, Missy!!" He looked at me reproachfully. "All the time you tell me, tell me that the American people have not got Neji. Now I see one in this American book."

Neji are the water people, much like human beings, who are supposed to live under the rivers in villages. They are said to demand mortals, especially red-haired ones, and will capsize a canoe to claim one. No native will defy the Neji by attempting to rescue a sandy-haired native, much less an auburn-haired white person.

"See, Missy!" Poor Boy brought the magazine over to me and pointed a trembling finger at the figure of a mermaid painted on the wall of a Hollywoodish bathroom.

"You see, Missy, the Neji is in her top part the same like a fine white woman. She has got long hair the color of gold like Missy Iversen. And the bottom part is same like a fish! It is a thing of much luck to me that I find this American Neji. Now it is not necessary for me to buy one."

"Buy one?" I exclaimed. "What are you talking about?"

"Sure, Missy, they are for sale," Poor Boy said patiently. "But not in the market. One man from Sierre Leone

has got a whole ship full, fresh from the United States,
up in Freetown. You pay this man the money; he buys
the Neji for you. You never see her. She will come in
the night while you sleep and leave money under your
bed blanket. She makes gold out of her hair. It is too
bad, Missy, that the fine hair that grows on your head is
black and not gold; otherwise Master might take some
to Research and make it into money. He would have
sense for this thing with all those glass bottles."

"Has anyone seen this Neji gold, Poor Boy?"

"Oh, yes, Missy! Plenty people see small gold already.
They tell all their friends. Then everyone puts his small
money together and gives it to the man. The price of a
Neji is twelve pounds [$48.00] same like a woman. After
next pay day the man will carry all the money to Sierre
Leone."

"And you will never see the man again," I said gloomily.

"That's all right, Missy," Poor Boy assured me confidently. "We will see the gold."

"Well," I said, "you will have as much luck with the
Neji you find in the American book as the people who
give money to the man. And now, suppose you get
money. What thing is your heart hungry for?"

"First," he said, "I will carry some of the gold to the
blacksmith and have some fine bangles made for Branca.
When her pickin is born, I will give them to her."

It was like a native to think of gold, first, in the light
of its beauty as a workable metal which makes bright
body adornment, rather than of its purchasing power.

"And after that, Poor Boy?"

"After, I will carry some to the dentist and have him make a coat for a tooth in the front of my mouth. You know, Missy, all your boys put their money together last pay, and buy one tooth that can come loose. Each is to wear it one day in turn. But the tooth fit only Johnny. Now he wears it all the time, as you have seen."

"And after the gold tooth, Poor Boy?"

"Then," he said, "I will buy some fine cloth." He pulled my husband's Palm Beach suit out of the laundry, and stroked the material with his slim fingers. "The talk of fine cloth to my hands is same like the talk of rice to my belly. It is for this that I am a washman. You know, Missy, that all your good friends bring their fine suits here for me to wash and they say that I can wash past all the boys on the plantation. I never ask dash. It is dash sufficient that fine cloth live for my hand. I like the talk of the suit that is like tree-bark, the big-man talk of the wool coat, the soft talk of the Missy underclothes that run over my hands like water over the rocks, the wool blanket that is like baby goats, the white curtain that is like having a cloud in my hands, the show-respect of the tablecloth that is stiff without starch. The only time I wish God had made me a white man is when I see how much fine cloth you have. I see in this book that all these things are plenty in your country." He pointed at an advertisement showing a movie actress nestled under a woolen blanket. On the opposite page was an advertisement for a washing machine.

"This, Poor Boy," I said, "is the washman in my country."

"Which way you like, Missy?" he asked.

"I like the Liberia way," I said. "A washing machine cannot tell me fine country stories while it does the work. And a washing machine cannot remember to bring me flowers for my hair when I go to a dinner."

He smiled. "Missy," he said, "I want to ask you something. How is it that when American medicine is so strong, when they can make fine things like castor oil, that all the people die young? I see no old people in this book."

"But no!" I said. "Our people live to be very old. My own father's ma and pa live at this time. They are almost ninety. That is the number you have if you call each rice-planting one ha'penny, and then you put down a shilling's worth of ha'pennies three times, and add ninepence to it."

Poor Boy was troubled.

"That is a number that is too great for me to put in my head," he said politely, "but if you will pay me in ha'pennies next moon, I will try to understand the great age of your people."

"You understand the number *blabwe*," I said. "Take it *mlennye* times."

"Missy" (he was reproachful again), "all the time you want me to learn times-es. *We do' like this way to count!* You tell me that two times two crawfish make four crawfish. All right, my eye sees that this is true, but my tongue does not agree. It is better to add one and one and one again with small stones. Then you have the feel of each stone in the hand, and if each stone means one crawfish, then you have the taste on the tongue of one crawfish for every stone in the hand."

"I can understand that," I said, "and I will not try to teach you times-es any more. Now I will tell you why all the women in the book look young. It is the custom in my country for a woman to try to look young no matter how many years she has. The people who make medicine for the face find that this is good business."

"I see," he said, "that many women in this book spend time putting medicine on the face. But this young idea is a great mistake. With our people, a woman is not shown much respect until she is old and has got sense with many rice-plantings. An old mamma will cost a man more to buy than a young frisky one."

"Some of our people have known the worth of an old mamma," I said. "We had one big man who was wise. His name was Ben Franklin. He was so wise that he took fire out of the sky, the thing we call lightning, and showed people it was electricity. This Ben Franklin wrote a small book on why it is better to have an old mamma."

"Ah," said Poor Boy, "I would like for you to tell me the story of how he caught the lightning, so I can tell the people in the camp. When he did this, he was not wise because sky-fire can bite; it has killed many of my people. In the women palaver, though, he had sense. When I get the new pickin that Branca is making now, I will call him Ben Franklin. That will be good medicine for sense, and good medicine against sky-fire."

"And if this sewing machine ever works again," I said, "I will make the pickin a shirt of fine cloth that you like so much."

"Castor oil will be good for both. I think it good for

you to send to the hospital for more oil. And now, there is another thing I do not understand about this book. How is it that your people make so many photo of small babies? Our people do not show respect to pickin. Photos are for chiefs and government people. It is just like this thing you call 'Christmas' when you get so busy and make such a hellova palaver over one small pickin called Jesus."

"That," I said, "is because of the respect we have for the man that Jesus became. With all our babies, we see in them the fine men they will become when they are grown."

"It would be better," he said, "to wait to see if they live. Plenty baby can die."

What he had said about babies dying was true. American doctors have estimated that the infant mortality rate in Liberia is between eighty and ninety per cent.

"Now this thing? What are these people doing?" He showed me a soap advertisement where a young couple were in the clinch of an amorous embrace because she had used, almost too late, the right kind of soap. "Our people do not do this thing," he went on scornfully. "It is a thing baboons do. Do you remember that when Master brought that old Town Chief home, all the little girl chimpanzees ran away in fear, save only Lucy, and she went up to him and put her mouth on his mouth, and now they stay together all the time? After I see this thing of Lucy and Town Chief, one time I see through the window that white people do this also. At the club on the night before the day of the New Year, I see all the people do it, when the hands on the clock stand up straight. I talk this with my people and they say, 'How is it that the Qui who have plenty sense in many things, in this man-woman business act like baboons?' "

By some coincidence, Ambrose who was still waiting mournfully by the door let out an emphatic "Oof!" Poor Boy filled the hollow of the iron with charcoal embers and caressed the Palm Beach suit into place on the ironing table. I struck up a thunderous rattle with the sewing machine over the greasy cloth which fumed of castor oil.

CHAPTER EIGHT

The Path Goes Under my Feet

AT LAST I was going to bush! I would know how it felt to walk under the big trees I had seen only from a distance. I would learn what things I would need for the long trip I wanted to make to Ganta. I would see how to manage the carriers. The path was going under my feet!

"Missy go for bush, today-o!" The houseboys sang the news over and over as they prepared the packs.

How many blankets would I need? Where was the canteen for boiled water? Where was the hammock I had borrowed from the cook?

"Missy go for bush today-o!"

Things! Things! When a native boy goes to visit his people he carries everything he owns on his head. No boiled water, no mosquito net, no tinned food, no coffeepot, no dishpan, no soap, no towels.

"Missy go to bush today-o. Oh, Missy-o!"

A raincoat, some matches, some salt. A cutlass, small coppers, the Flit! Things! Things!

Johnny must slice the long bar of blue soap into inch-long cakes. Soap and matches to dash the little chiefs, salt and tobacco for the big chiefs. Corned beef at one shilling four. Expensive! Eight o'clock! Hurry-o!

Poor Boy was appointed overseer. He portioned out the loads and carried the gun and lantern. Pickles, the dog, walked ahead of me in the procession, stopping without warning to smell the trail just where my foot was about to descend. Our path was narrow between "low bush" higher than our heads. Vines reached out toward each other across the path. A few days of disuse and it would be matted shut. The sun was hot.

On, on, hotter, hotter, on, on! On, on, and on!

We came to a village, finally. Pickles chased the village goats which scattered, bleating. Babies playing in the dust of the bare earth between the huts bellowed in terror. Mammas came to the rescue, lifted their children by one arm, and stared at us. The village dogs chased Pickles, a whole pack of them. Goats, babies, dogs, all howling. The heat seemed to amplify the noises. Surely nothing could sound so loud in the dewy freshness of early morning. I took the gun and lantern so that Poor Boy could carry Pickles. He held her by one leg just out of reach of her yelping pursuers.

On, on. The boiled water in the canteen tasted sickishly tepid. I was getting a blister.

We came to a swamp which I wanted to wade. But, no! Infection in raw blisters! It could be serious. Poor Boy tossed me on his back easily, as though I had been a sack of rice, and carried me "piggy-back" through the mire.

Swamp behind, hill ahead! The boys became strangely

quiet. We passed a woven mat wall, higher than our heads.

"Devil bush, Missy! Don't put your eye there. The one who tries to see can die-o!"

Buno and Fine Boy had each spent four years behind such a wall. There they received the elaborate decoration of raised scars on their beautiful backs, "cuts that hurt so bad, it be better to die than to have such again-o." By the Devil's marks, he can know them; he has had his tribute of pain, he cannot catch them again. But suppose the Devil should catch a Bassau boy, Poor Boy or Johnny, on the trail and put the marks of the crocodile teeth in his back? That boy cannot go again to his people.

"Missy, I beg you, put your eye away from the wall." I was forgetting to keep my head averted.

"Suppose I see small hole in the wall," I whispered to Buno. "I meet the Devil-eye through the small hole. What then?"

"The eye that meet the Devil can't see more again," said Buno with a shiver. "Missy, I *beg* you, look so for the other side."

We were far beyond the mat wall before the chatter began again.

On, on. My cork helmet pressed my head down. How did the boys manage to hold their heads high beneath forty-pound loads? I exchanged the helmet for a double felt. Poor Boy perched the helmet on top of the box on top of his head.

All my clothes were soaked with perspiration. Sometimes a small breeze blew through them and they became almost dry. I steamed like a laundry in front of a hot oven.

Pickles continued to stop in front of me without warning. When I stopped suddenly the end of my blistered toe hit the end of my shoe which seemed to be getting increasingly shorter. I wished that Pickles would get lost in the bush. I wished that the Kpuesi people would have fine dog-chop that night.

On, hot, on, hot! My will reiterated the "on," my tired soft body, for which I was rapidly losing respect, was echoing the "hot."

Finally, we came to a flowing stream. The boys stacked their loads and rushed in, bathing and drinking all at once. They lapped from their cupped hands in gulps. I took a mouthful of the flat warm stuff in my canteen and spat it out in disgust. My tongue was cottony. I watched the boys take mouthfuls of the cool water in the stream and spout it out of their mouths in crystal geysers.

On the trail again. We crossed a swamp on single poles, laid end to end. Buno walked ahead of me with a big basket on his head. He seemed to glide rather than walk and never touched the basket on his head. I minced along uncertainly. Once when I swayed and almost fell, he reached back and took my hand to steady me. Even with my swaying weight pulling at him, he had no need to touch the basket. It stayed on his head as though it had grown there.

We reached a rather large town on the bank of a river about the middle of the afternoon. It seemed a good place to spend the night. I went to stand before the chief.

Chief Tchukol lay in a hammock stretched across the

piazza of a big mud hut. He was dressed in a khaki tunic and ancient black trousers. On his small head he wore an embroidered black pillbox hat. His bare feet sticking out of the hammock toward us were small and neat. They went with the small, crafty-looking head and delicate hands. He greeted me in English, but used the Mohammedan gesture of touching his heart.

We stood while elaborate compliments were exchanged on both sides. I spoke of the clean streets, the fat babies, the many goats, the many houses. Finally, I asked him for a place where I could change into my swimming clothes and later, sleep for the night. He indicated the big palaver house in the center of the town. He would not hear any palavers until next moon and the finest place in the town should be for me. The palaver house was a great cone-shaped roof held aloft with carved poles. The encircling mud wall was not more than two feet high! In one end, a throne for the chief had been rubbed with white clay and decorated with sweeps of the hand in the wet mud. It was a fine structure, but hardly a dressing room.

A big tree along the bank might be the solution. I set off for the river with most of the village following. Pickles was again involved with the village dogs, and we had frightened a number of children.

At the river's edge, I discovered a large mud hut which the owner was glad to let me have for the night. I went inside and shut the heavy wooden door. There were several small rooms. I entered one and shed my steaming clothing. How wonderful to be rid of my clothing, to be comfortably nude. I yawned and stretched.

Some sound caused me to look at the outside wall. There on the hillside opposite was a great host of people watching me through the window hole. I dived into my bathing suit in an embarrassed flurry, while the crowd laughed.   Several old women came to the door and pushed their way inside. They felt of my hair and legs and breasts and the muscle in my forearm.

"Ma," said one of them, "you grow long past all we, but you got small-girl front for true." She pointed a derisive finger at my breasts, and looked proudly at her own which hung to her waist.

"So God make white woman-part," said another. "Go now. Leff the ma for take baph."

"How the white woman can put on cloth for take baph?" said the first old crone, and laughed at the good joke of it.

Poor Boy made coffee and I drank it sitting in the river up to my neck.

Back at the hut I found my hammock suspended from the lacing of poles across the top of the mud-room partitions. I stretched out and reveled in a drowsy feeling of complete well-being. How good to be clean and cool and horizontal after having been none of these for so many hours. I was completely exhausted, yet our trek had been a short day's walk. I would have to toughen up before I started on the long trip to Ganta.

The sunlight came through little holes in the thatch roof, and dust particles danced crazily in the pencil-like beams of light. In one of these shafts, directly above me, was something brilliant yellow green. Not until it moved did I realize there was a snake on the rafter above my hammock. I think I screamed. At least the scream was in my throat; I am not sure it broke through the frozen horror of my fear.

Poor Boy came at my call and dislodged the snake with a long pole. It met a hasty and applauded end on the floor.

"Green mamba!" said Poor Boy. "That one can live in trees and in thatch. He can hunt people. If it bite person, that person can die-o. It good to put fire in house before Missy lie down. Snake can't like plenty smoke, so he say, 'All right, the Ma come, I go, yah.'"

"After this we will always build a fire before we lie down in a house," I said.

"Yeah, Missy, I make fire, just now. Sometime plenty snake can stay for the thatch. No rats this time, though. Snakes chop the rats."

I walked to the village to talk to the chief while the boys cooked our supper. Tchukol was persuaded to show me his women's quarters. The house was a huge mud affair, and seemed to consist of several separate mud huts opening into a center court, the whole covered by a single huge thatch roof.

The chief had one of the rooms in the establishment for his own. It contained a wide hand-carved bed covered with country cloth and mosquito net. Bamboo mats carpeted the mud floor.

The headwife's room was almost as large as the chief's own and similarly furnished.

In the center court there were many narrow beds without mattresses set in dormitory rows. Cooking pots and rice mortars stood about. Chickens and goats passed freely in and out. Several babies played together on a bamboo mat.

"How can you keep palaver out of a house of many women?" I asked the chief.

"Sometimes palaver comes under this roof," admitted Tchukol. "But the women must live under the law. All the women with small pickin to take milk and all the women with pickin in the belly, these I do not sleep with. Few remain. I have one in turn each night in the chief-bed. All the other women and all the children sleep for the center part."

Tchukol "called a play" for my entertainment that night. A Devil came to dance for us. The chief and a visiting Gola chief and I sat on chairs around a table outside the chief's house. The drums tuned up gradually and the people gathered in front of us. They began to shuffle and then to move in a circle. One dancer took position in the center of the circle. The drums played faster. The center dancer whirled, leaped, rolled on the ground, sprang up again, moved his feet faster and faster, while the slowly moving circle around him chanted and shuffled and swayed. When he was finally exhausted he rolled out of the circle and another took his place.

Someone placed a naked child on my lap. He bounced with the drum rhythm. During a lull in the dancing, his father gave him to me as casually as one might give away a kitten. While I was trying to think of a diplomatic refusal, the Play Devil entered with a great fanfare of wooden horns and bells. He wore a long-necked black mask which reached down over his head to his shoulders. His costume was layers and layers of raffia, so that he resembled an animated haystack. Never once in all his twisting or turning did I catch a glimpse of hands or feet. He was the height of two men when he entered, but at moments of great activity he would suddenly shrink to ordinary height, then become tall again. He turned somersaults and cartwheels. Finally he sank in the dust, a weary heap of grass, rose again, and whirled away like a tumbleweed in the wind. How could he grow, and shrink, and grow again? Were my eyes playing tricks? Perhaps he used stilts; I do not know. It was all very rapid and confusing. I have never seen more fascinating entertainment.

The dancing was over when almost everyone present had had his turn in the center of the circle, worked himself into an ecstatic frenzy, and, foaming at the mouth, had finally collapsed and rolled out of the group between the moving feet of those who were still able to participate. There was no drinking of palm wine or cane juice. This was a Mohammedan tribe and they do not drink. The intoxication was drum-made and sexual. One expected the great wall of jungle behind the village to pulsate; the earth beneath our feet carried the beat-pattern.

The spent dancers lay where they had made their final flop, in the grotesque postures of those who die violent deaths. The twitching of a bronzed muscle in the moonlight, a low moan heard in the drum pauses, and they were corpselike again.

The night was far spent when Tchukol signaled for festivities to stop. The child which had been given me was sleeping heavily in my arms. Having no idea where his father had gone nor how to return this gift if I did find him, I shoved him at the first woman to pass me on her way to her hut. She took the child without question and he groped sleepily for one of her swaying nipples.

Eight children got under the table at which I had sat with the chiefs, and began to dance with it on their heads. Only their flying black legs showed under the light top as they went down the road ahead of us. The tired drummers followed the children. Tchukol and the Gola chief walked on either side of me, their palms cupped on my elbows. The villagers who were still able to stand walked behind us. It was a ludicrous moonlight procession. When they reached the house by the river, it was evident that the chiefs expected to be invited in. Tchukol stood in front of the open door and I could not pass him without making an issue of the matter.

"Good night," I said.

"Good night, Ma," said Tchukol, without budging.

"Good night, Ma," said the Gola chief.

"Good night," I said a little more loudly.

"Good night, Ma," they both said again, without giving ground. The drummers had set up their drums on the piazza and were beating out a lazy rhythm, the way they do before tuning up for a long session. I looked at the crowd around the porch. They seemed expectant. Not one of my own boys was in sight.

"Good night!" I shouted, and gauged the space between the doorjamb on either side of the firmly planted Tchukol. I might lower my head and charge through, but what if the door had no latch or I couldn't close it before Tchukol barged in? There was a determined glint in his eye. No, it was better to keep him out on the piazza in plain view of the villagers. I would stand there the rest of the night if necessary.

"You are a fine ma," said Tchukol in a greasy voice.

I stared coldly past my persistent escort and made no reply. If only I hadn't let him maneuver into the doorway! Where were my carriers? My gun and all the luggage were inside and they were supposed to guard it. Had the Bassaus been frightened and run back to the plantation?

"I am tired, Chief Tchukol, and want to sleep," I had to shout now to be heard above the rising drums.

"But first, Ma —— "

I didn't hear the rest. Framed in the doorway behind the chief was the dim outline of a sleepy Poor Boy.

"Excuse, please, Chief." Poor Boy made his way toward me with a packing case in his hand, the one containing the dashes.

"I think, Missy, that the thing the chief wait for is dash from your hand."

I gave him the first things to come out of the case, several bandannas, a sack of Epsom salts, some bars of soap, and a string of shiny safety pins.

"You are a fine ma," he said again, but this time he said it from the piazza step!

"I'd like you to sleep across the foot of my door, Poor Boy." I was unnerved and very weary.

Finally in my hammock, I swept the walls of the room with my flashlight. The beam picked up a ruby-red eye. The eye was set in a spider, big as a saucer, which Poor Boy killed with his bare hand.

In the morning when it was just light enough to tell a red string from a white string, I was awakened by the long-drawn musical Moslem prayer call. It was dream-like in the cool dawn.

After coffee, I floated down the river in a canoe. It was made from the trunk of a great tree, hollowed out until the sides were less than an inch thick. I sat in the usual African canoe posture, on my haunches in the bottom. It was a good canoe; my bottom was dry.

One boy sat in the stern and softly crooned a Vai song. It is a lovely language, soft like Spanish instead of the thick-lipped consonant-ridden speech of some of the tribes.

The most handsome native boy I had ever seen stood in the prow. He wore a long flowing robe of blue and white country cloth which rippled in the breeze. His paddle was an almond-shaped, carved blade on the end of a long pole.

Brilliant birds were taking their morning baths. The trees were like a dream of forest. Some were heavy with bloom. Some were laced with vines. Many had ferns and orchids growing on the limbs. Great roots as high as small trees which had been washed free of soil during raging torrents hung stiffly toward the water like long cadaverous fingers. We passed a tree hung full of monkeys doing acrobatics. Blossoms fell from the trees and trailed our canoe. The Vai song lifted and fell with the paddle. The bronze god standing in the prow turned and asked me if my heart told me this was good.

CHAPTER NINE

A Head Grows Proper

FROM THE DAY I discovered that the wood in the wood-box was solid mahogany, I longed to try it under my chisel. Except for a few experimental chips, I had to wait until a carpenter could be found to make a work bench, and until a palaver-house studio could be built.

The work bench started with the live tree, standing in the bush. Willie Sawyer and his brother Moses took a day to explore for something they called "black gum," which makes good planks. They took me to the tree when they had found it, hacking a path through the dense undergrowth with a cutlass. Saw grass cut through the sleeves of my shirt and laced my arms with narrow gashes. The leather of my shoes was cut through by the razor edges. The double-pronged barbs of the climbing palms caught into my flesh and held me helpless as a fish until I released myself. Yet, Willie and Moses walked ahead of me barefooted and without clothing except for brief loin aprons, and they were unscathed.

"It be a way of walking, Ma," Willie told me. "When Ma walks, she go ahead with force the whole time. So walk all your people. It be the United States way. The

111

grass catch you, and hurt you the whole length of the leaf. We-part can't fight the leaf so, we let the leaf bend we; we no bend the leaf. Sit down small, Ma, and I tell you country story.

"This story tell how sense came to we. The story belong to the people who call God Allah. One Vai man who sit down in Pa's town to weave cloth for the chief tell it to we.

"One man live for the far north country in old time. That man ca' no' vex easy. When the rice birds carry his rice he say, 'No mind, yah?' When the fever catch him, he lie down easy in his hammock and hang his head in good thought, and he say, 'All bad thing can finish some time.' When his wife vex for his easy ways and make trouble for him and go back to her people and the people refuse to pay him back the bride-price, he say, 'Let the woman go. I will buy me one woman with easy ways.' So he buy him a fine Vai woman who never make big-mouth.

"One day the man go to big bush for shoot meat and he meet a jinni. The jinni say to the man, 'Dash me the meat you shoot.'

"The man with good ways give him the meat, and the jinni say, 'Now what thing you want from my hand?'

"The man say, 'I like to get a man-pickin with sense.'

"So the man go to his village and tell his wife, and she say, 'All right, let us make pickin.' And the pickin came good, and had sense past all the small boys in the town.

"One day the man said to his small-boy, 'I like to get more sense. Where can I look to know more?'

"And the small-boy who know plenty thing past the old man say, 'Look to God. Sense comes from God.'

"So the man went on a long journey to fin' God. He look, he look, he look ti' he tire. Plenty time the man lie down to sleep with empty belly because he give the meat he shoot to all who ask. He look in the sea, he look in the grass of the Mandingo country, he look in the hills, but he never see God. After many rice-plantings passed he find God in the big bush while he sleep.

"God say, 'I try you hard, good man. Person can no' find God until he look long time. Now I bring you sense for all your people.'

"When the man awoke, there was a big Vai basket covered with banana leaves, and the man was glad in his heart and started to carry the basket of sense back to his people. He walk many days and the rain catch him and the sun catch him, and when he come to the big water, he have to swim with the basket on his head.

"Finally he hear the rice mortars from his own town, and he try to walk strong to reach soon. Plenty vines cross the path and catch him and the saw grass cut him so the blood run from him. But he can't care for hurt. Then one big vine with small knives that grow from it catch the basket of sense and hold tight and the man cry.

"Then his small-boy, the pickin with sense, come on the path and meet his pa and see the trouble.

" 'Go back small,' said the small-boy, 'and then bend your head. When you bend your head sufficient you can pass.'

"And so it was, Missy. The man could pass. But he

vex because he himself did not know this small thing. He vex so he throw the Vai basket on the ground and it break, and it make great sound like the thunder when the dry-time finish and the rain come, and all the sense run like water on the ground. The small-boy fell to the ground and try to catch small sense in his hand, and all the people in the village hear the big sound and come one-time and try to catch small, but most of the sense stay in the big bush, and our people go in the bush to this day to look for sense from God."

Willie did not say, "The moral of this fable is . . . " There was no need. Take time, remember to bend the head. . . .

When we reached the tree, the salty perspiration that was streaming from my every pore smarted in the fret-work of gashes that covered my body. I sat down wearily on a log while Willie talked to the great tree in Bush Bassau.

"What's the one you are talking, Willie?"

"I make a begging to the tree, Missy. I tell the tree I sorry too much to put axe to the tree, Missy. I tell the tree that Missy need him. I say the Missy got good heart for everything that live, and she can have good ways for the wood. When the wood live for the Missy house, it heart can lay down good."

I coveted for the people of my country this feeling for a living tree. If a "begging from the heart" were made to every tree before it was cut in the United States . . .

When the great tree began to topple, it was held aloft by the tangle of vines that had used it as a support to climb to the sunlight of the jungle ceiling. The mighty trunk which had been nourishment to these great knotted and twisted and flattened cables was for the moment sustained by them.

"Missy, look!" exclaimed Willie. "For long time, the tree hold the vine so he can see the sun. The vine take his chop from the tree. He no ask; he just take, same like Liberian government man take from we. Now the vine, he hold the tree for the first time, but it be the last time also, for the tree, he die. So it can be with we — long time in front of now."

When the swaying weight of the tree had torn the anchor of vines and lay on the ground it was amazingly large. The Bassaus have a saying, "Do not measure your tree in the jungle."

"Plenty good friend have to help we carry the stick high," said Willie, appraising its great girth. "Today we build the saw stand and make the small kitchen for cook chop while we work."

The saw stand was a framework of logs built to support a twelve-foot section of the tree horizontally, about eight feet above the ground. It stood on its spread legs like an unwieldy new-born colt. It was propped and re-propped and tied together with jungle vines.

The kitchen was a sparse thatch roof held up by two short poles in the back, and two longer ones in front. It was just large enough for a man to squat in beside a small cooking fire.

The next day a host of Willie's country brothers came to help him roll the section of log up onto the saw stand. They made an inclined ramp of poles from the ground to the bed of the saw frame. Then, with much grunting, moaning, sweating, and Bush Bassau cursing, to the accompaniment of a lift song of "Zhey! Hozhey! Zhey! Hozhey! Zhey!" the huge log was rolled into place.

Willie ground charcoal in a broken latex cup, made a paste of it with water, and wallowed raffia string in the black mass until it was completely covered. Then he and Moses held the string taut at the ends of the log, and flipped straight lines at about two-inch intervals. When the whole log had been marked off with saw lines, they were ready to work.

Willie stood on top of the log and lifted the blade of their long saw. Moses stood on the ground beneath and pulled down, assisted by gravity. The arch of Willie's back was the arc of a circle, continuously redrawn against the green jungle backdrop. The steel blade of the saw moved forward. The rhythm of their motion flowed through their glistening bodies.

Willie and Moses cut good planks and made good talk when they stopped to rest and cook small chop in the kitchen. From the time that the pepper bird made his loud talk until the sun "sat down small" on the dead trees on the western hill, Willie and Moses lived with their work.

While they shared their roast cassava with me around the small kitchen fire, Willie told me about his pa who "could cut stick past all people."

"My-part work in the land of my people," I told him, "is also to cut stick. I like to see the way your pa can do."

"Tomorrow-time," Willie promised, "I bring you small thing from the hand of Chief Kondea, my pa."

The thing he brought me was a wooden rice spoon, smooth as satin, beautifully proportioned and balanced.

"How Kondea can make the wood smooth like the stone that live for the river?" I asked.

"Hah, Ma, you don't know that one? I show you." He was off to the bush and brought back a handful of leaves. The undersides were rough with thorny prickles.

"That one fine country sandpaper," he said. "When God make the world he make plenty thing for the people who cut stick."

The palaver-house studio progressed as slowly as the work bench. The poles for the uprights and roof were brought from the bush, and the palm thatch for the cone-shaped roof was laid in a long cord, but there was no rattan with which to tie the thatch onto the roof poles.

While I waited through the delays, I sorted all the wood beneath the house, and stacked the largest solid pieces in a separate pile. I wanted to find a typical and characteristic head-type in each of the different tribes. Already I could identify most of the tribesmen by their head shapes and facial characteristics. But I wanted to make something more than a record of head contours, something more than portraits of individuals. I wanted to say something in wood about the lean weeks when the supply of rice in the rice kitchens is finished and the new crop has not yet come in; something about the patience with which native people fight the jungle; something about the quick joy that possesses a face when the dance drums throb; something of the reverence with which they listen to the wind.

"Fire must not catch this part," I told Buno Yardboy when I had sorted out the best wood.

Later, I heard Buno tell one of his Kpuesi brothers under the house, "This-part wood be Missy-stick. The boy that chop Missy-stick can catch hell-o."

"What thing the Missy do with the stick?" asked the visitor.

"Well, I can't say," said Buno. "But it be some kind of cut-stick palaver. I hear the people say the Missy can cut boys' head in wood."

"Sometime," the Kpuesi boy mused, "maybe the white woman can want to make bad medicine for we."

I knew that when a native medicine man wants to make bad medicine against someone he abuses a clay image of the victim. Would I be able to persuade anyone to model for me? I used every opportunity to make my intentions clear to the servants.

"It is a photo I make in the stick," I told them. "Boss make photo with the black box; Missy make the photo with chisel and wood. When I see boy with fine, fine head, I make photo in wood."

Wheager was my first model. I first saw his tattered petunia-colored shirt rippling in the evening breeze while I stood at a window admiring the purples and reds of a sunset. It was as though a few shreds of colored cloud had been torn from the heavens by one of the stark branches of the big dead trees on the horizon, and had floated down to me. Above the fluttering shirt was an old, yellow American straw hat. The top of the crown was taking leave of the straight sides, so that as Wheager bounced along he was not only shaded, but also fanned, by the flopping circle of straw.

"Who lives under the hat?" I sent Johnny to find out.

"The hat live for the head of one boy named Robert Wheager Fisher Yardboy," reported Johnny. "He say God tell him come do yardboy work for the Missy."

Wheager had two interests: keeping his stomach full, and remembering the happy days he had spent with Mr. Fisher.

When Mr. Fisher went back to the States and gave Wheager his old straw hat, it was just like God letting

out one of the heavenly halos for mortal headgear. Mr.
Fisher and God were both "beeg, beeg" men in Wheager's estimation, but God did not have a pickup to carry
Wheager around the plantation. Now that Mr. Fisher
was back in the United States, they were equally remote,
but Mr. Fisher had promised Wheager that some day he
would come back and Wheager could be his boy again.
Mr. Fisher had good ways, and a "goo' heart" and laughed
plenty, but Wheager wasn't so sure about God. He had
heard God vex in the thunder, but he had never seen
God's belly shake with laughter.

Wheager vexed my coast Bassaus with his aversion for
soap and water.

"Wheager is a Bush Bassau," Johnny explained, "and
those people can't care for clean. All your other Bassau
boys take three hot bath every day. Even the Kpuesi
people take bath past Wheager. Sometimes water can't
touch Wheager for a whole week together."

Sammi didn't want Wheager in his kitchen. None of
the boys would let him sit on their beds. But when
Wheager sat on the grass and told them stories about his
pa, and about Mr. Fisher, they rolled with laughter.
Wheager was the court jester, a little gnome with knobby
knees whose only contribution to the world was to make
everyone around him laugh. Before beginning a story,
Wheager always gathered up the tattered ribbons of his
purple shirt which once had been the top part of
one of Mr. Fisher's pajamas, stuffed the bulk of his silken
rags into his negligible trousers, and affectionately patted
the result. Then the story went on with elaborate gestures. Afterward when I tried to write down his tales,

they did not seem good. Like the gift without the giver, Wheager's stories, without Wheager, were bare.

When the water was to be carried, Wheager was out looking for sweet potatoes. When there was wood to be chopped, Wheager was in the swamp hunting for bullfrogs. When the animal food was to be cooked, Wheager was gone to find cassava. He would eat his week's ration of rice in two days, and spend the other five hunting food.

The more I saw of Wheager's impish face with its amazing prognathous jaw, the more certain I was that I wanted him for my first model. I explained to him that I wanted to make his photo in wood and all he needed to do was to sit still for a long time. This seemed to strike him as a pleasing occupation for which he was suited by temperament.

"I will wear my new trouser for the photo," he said.

"But the photo I make is for the head part only. Trouser can't show in this one."

"Oh, Missy, the trouser can show!" he said. "When a boy got new trouser, the heart can grow big with glad. And when the heart be glad, the glad can show in the face. So, you see, the trouser can show."

"But where you get new trouser?" I asked. "You never take pay from my hand, because the moon never finish, this time."

"Missy, one man die in my pa's town," said Wheager, happily. "This man, he leff his trouser to me. It is necessary I walk one day to reach my people. That night, my people give me plenty rice, and I sleep for the town. Soon morning, I come again with the trouser in my hand."

When Wheager appeared in my living room with his inheritance rolled in a tight gray bundle under his arm, I gave him blue soap and sent him to the creek to beat the garment on the washing rock, wondering of what horrible disease his benefactor had died.

"Soap and rock can make new cloth fini soon," objected Wheager.

"Dirty trouser can make yardboy work fini soon," I said sternly.

When the gray pants came back from the creek they were, to my surprise and Wheager's delight, cream-colored with a black pin-stripe. They added greatly to his sartorial impressiveness.

Johnny shook his head over my choice of a model.

"Missy," he said, "it is true that Wheager got fine shirt, fine trouser, fine American hat, but Wheager got awkward face."

"It be the Wheager laugh that I want in the Wheager head," I said.

"It true that laugh grow in Wheager past all people," grudgingly admitted Johnny. "But he can laugh the whole time because he can't care for nothing. Myself, I take care for the dust under the chair, I take care for the press in Missy's clothes, I take care for the way I dress the table, and too much take-care can dry the laugh, same way like dry-time sun carry the water from the river."

"Johnny," I said, "I like you because you take care, and I like Wheager because he makes the house laugh. Because I like you both, equal, what matter the why I like you?"

He went away with his face tied in thought, and began

to polish the silver. That night, I found a small hair in my soup. My husband found a similar one in his. I called Johnny.

"Johnny, you been barbered today?"

"No, Missy."

"Maybe Sammi been barbered. You tell all the boys that so soon they finish being barbered, they must stand under the boys' shower bath long time, so the water can carry all the small hair from the head. Hair live for my soup tonight, and for Boss part also, and I can no agree for that one. It vex me plenty!"

Johnny's eyes filmed with tears.

"Don't vex, Missy. And I beg you, don't sack me. All we, we know the shower palaver. This one, some different thing."

"What kind of different thing?"

"Missy, my hair be part me, so I put that part me inside the soup. When you and Massio eat that one, and find it good, you can have good heart for me, you can like me same way you like Wheager." His face began to twitch, pulled by the low sobs in his throat.

"Johnny, we like you fine," my husband said. "To-morrow-time, I take my black photo box, and make fine photo of you. You wash the new uniform with the shiny buttons that Missy tailor for you, you put plenty starch inside, you iron him proper. Ah hah, the photo can be fine past the Wheager head self. — With apologies to you for the brief triumph of photography over the fine arts," he added in an aside to me.

"Yeah, Boss. Thank you plenty, Boss." The vertical lines of trouble relaxed into curved smile-wreaths.

"But no more small-part you in the chop! You hear that one good?"

"Yeah, Boss."

As the Wheager head grew, Wheager talked to it constantly. He gave it detailed instructions about how to behave. He seemed to think of it as a sort of other self that might bring him into palavers.

"Sometime," he told the head, "when you do all good thing and no bad, you can wear Mr. Fisher's hat for small time. And when Mr. Fisher come back to Wheager, and there be two Wheager, oh, Mr. Fisher can laugh."

When I had the mouth blocked out, he announced, "Now the head ready to take chop. Let me go find small chop for the head. It can no grow proper without small chop."

The head demanded increasing amounts of food to "grow proper" as the work progressed. Several stalks of bananas, many lengths of sugar cane, and a few unfortunate snakes, rats, and bullfrogs were consumed.

Wheager looked at the finished carving for a long time, and finally announced, "It be Wheager for true."

"Yes," I agreed, "it be Wheager, for true, because it eat past all."

"Oh, Missy," groaned Wheager. "I hungry till I die-o just now."

I was sanding the head the day Willie Sawyer brought his pa, Chief Kondea, to the palaver house to meet me. Kondea wore a fine blue-and-white country-cloth chief robe. He carried a chief's scepter and walked with great dignity. We snapped fingers many times, and I repeated

over and over, "Moin, Pa, Moin!" while he repeated,
"Moin, Ma, Moin!"

Then he saw the head. The surprised roar that came
out of his throat was like rushing wind over the river before a storm. He talked out his excitement to Willie,
and then stood with his mouth open, ready to talk again
when he recovered from his amazement.

"What thing Kondea say, Willie?"

"He say the head be fine, same like the boy. He say
he know that boy. The boy's pa be country brother to
Kondea. He live one-day walk across the river."

Kondea recovered the use of his fallen jaw and talked
to Willie again. Then he laughed and held his sides
against his laughter, and Willie laughed, too.

"What your pa say, now, Willie?"

"Pa say the head be ready to talk and when it can
speak it can beg for chop. Pa know the ways of that boy
too much."

Willie then showed me "the small-part dash" he had
brought to me. It was a dozen white sticks, about an
inch wide at one end and tapered to a pinpoint on the
other end. The points had been charred to make them
smooth. On the wider end of each, a geometric design
had been carved in the wood and burned. Each design
was handsome and different from each of the others.

"What thing these, Willie?"

"Country hairpin, Ma."

I twisted my hair into a knot and pinned it in place
with all of the twelve pins, while Kondea and Willie
beamed.

"What small thing you like for your-part dash?" I asked Willie, who consulted with his pa.

"The chief say," said Willie, "that he like to come every day when the ma cut stick and learn her-part work."

"I agree," I said. "And myself, I like to watch Kondea do his-part work. But now I give you one piece American bread for the dash part."

Kondea picked up the Wheager head and felt it carefully as though he saw with his hands. He let out one last grunt of surprise before he went away. I watched him go down the trail to his village shaking his head.

That evening when the living room was filled with guests who had come to dinner, we had an impromptu unveiling of the head. I was not entirely pleased with my work. The head was an image of Wheager, but it was too much Wheager in good behavior. The gnome of the forest had not been caught in the wood. Perhaps Wheager had talked too much to the head about the proper way to behave.

Many days later, Lieutenant Fisher, resplendent in navy whites, stopped at the plantation on a flight to a new naval assignment. He came to our house.

"Your last name is God, you like purple pajamas, you once had a shirt green as the jungle, and you like to eat lunch on a hot day with your feet up on a small table and plenty of salami and beer close at hand," I said.

"Stop!" he said, "you frighten me. Where did you find out all that, and don't tell me what else you know."

"Robert Wheager Fisher Yardboy," I said and pointed at the head.

"Good old Wheager!" Jimmy Fisher laughed just the way Wheager had said he would, and patted the wooden head. Then he placed his gleaming officer's cap at a jaunty angle on the head, and sat down to talk.

The Wheager head wore a Mr. Fisher hat! But little old Wheager was not there to see this fine thing happen. Wheager had gone to his father's village to beg a little rice.

"If Wheager had more take-care for his work in his heart, he would be here to see his goo' friend," asserted Johnny.

Before I started another head, I spent many days in Kondea's village watching him carve, learning what woods were best, where to find the trees in the jungle, which ones to carve wet and which ones to season. One day he brought up the subject of the Wheager head. Willie interpreted for us.

"The chief say," said Willie, "that the photo you make of Wheager be fine, but if the chief make the photo of Wheager in wood, he will make it all belly."

I wished that Kondea could explain modern art to all my friends who scoffed at distortion.

CHAPTER TEN

Wooden Bowls and Spoons

ONE MORNING when I slept late, Johnny announced that one of my friends waited on me under the house and he thought I would want to get up because the man had brought me a fine thing.

The visitor was old Chief Kondea and the thing he had brought was a wooden rice bowl. It was oval at one end and pointed at the other, with flared sides so that it resembled the hull of a toy ship. The white wild-rubber wood had been rubbed to a high gloss and the rim was decorated with a geometric design burned with a hot wire. It was as large as an ordinary vegetable serving dish, which is just the right size for an individual serving of country chop.

Johnny looked at it and said it would be just the right size for Sunday country chop for the master, but that our friend Mr. Burgess would need one twice as large, and that Mr. Dendel who cared little for rice would need a smaller one at his place at table.

"Tell the chief, Johnny, that I would like to buy many bowls to use at Sunday table, one for each of our friends who come here every time. You can tell the chief the

way each man likes rice, and when he carves he will
know for which man's part he makes the bowl."

This was the kind of humor which both Johnny and
Kondea thoroughly enjoyed. All the servants gathered
around while Johnny gave a half-hour pantomime showing all the mannerisms, the ways of lighting cigarettes,
the ways of refusing or accepting second helpings, of each
of our friends. Even if I had not understood their Bassau
names, I would have known who was being delineated.
The Bishop had a name which meant "God-palaver-
man," and his bowl must be rather large. My husband's
name meant "the man who saves everything," and because he always ate everything on his plate, his bowl
might be a little smaller than the others.

Old Kondea roared with laughter (a thing I had not
heard him do for many days because he had many troubles at this time) and said that he would make the bowls,
but that the one he had brought that morning must be
for me because I had lived in his head while he cut it
with his hands.

I did not see Kondea again for many days, although
he was in the habit of coming several times a week to
watch me carve. I wondered whether he were hard at
work on my bowls or whether he were sitting idly by the
river trying to discover answers to the problems which
beset him.

One Sunday morning when the sun was a red ball in
the morning sky, and the water in the river boiled over
the rocks and flung back heated spray, the humid air
seemed to slow my chisels before they struck the wood I
carved. It was one of those mornings when the air is so

thick with heat and moisture that the whole continent seems to be breathing in the labored fashion of a heavy, sick person. I stacked my chisels and started off to see my good friend Kondea.

The leaves of the rubber trees along the path to Kondea's town looked waxy-warm as though they too were perspiring. As I left the rubber and went down a steep incline into the big bush, it was like descending a tunnel into a damp, subterranean world. The light that filtered through the ceiling of leaves was a blue-green reflection of the glare in the sky above. The trunks of the big trees were great black cylinders rising in the gloom of a surrealistic dream. The waxy leaves of a small creeping plant reached toward each other across the moss on the foot-wide path. There was a flash on iridescent peacock-blue as a large plaintain eater winged through the trees.

I turned off the path by the great Spirit Tree and crept through a tunnel of foliage until I reached the high stone altar, set in a niche between the buttress roots of the mighty bombax tree.

Seen from the side which is toward the river, the Spirit Tree presents a giant and fantastic stage-set arrangement. The backdrop is a rounded hill covered with moss and purplish boulders. It towers above the other jungle which is made up of trees with weirdly twisted aerial roots, out of which mossy vines droop in layers like stage wings. The spot seems older than anything on earth. It's as though God sat there and twisted one of the vines in His fingers while he thought up the Creation. The supporting buttress roots of the Spirit Tree are twenty or more feet high, and one of them curves as it tapers off along the ground, forming a great protecting arm around the flat circle of earth where the stone altar is set.

A phalluslike formation of clay had been placed on the rock altar, and there were dishes for sacrifice. Here the women of Kondea's town came with white rice and white chickens to perform their rites in front of the clay symbol and pray for children. Here in a man-high niche where the snaking buttress roots join the trunk of the tree, old Kondea should be stood when he is dead, and a great stone rolled in front of him to seal his tomb. But the land had gone to the plantation, and the spirit of the chief would never be given its proper home. This was the great sadness which was continually upon him these days. He felt that his spirit could not rest in the new town.

The coffee trees around the village had been felled since my last visit. I met Willie Sawyer, Kondea's son, on the trail and asked him about it.

"You see, Ma," explained Willie, "it is so we can no claim the land. Where there stands a tree that a man has planted or that a man's father has planted, that land belongs to the man, no matter what the law say. It be God-law that a man owns where his hand has planted seed. One policeman stay for the town so no seed fall from our hand."

"What time you must go for the new town across the river?"

"My pa say we can no go until the Devil school has finished," said Willie. "And this time it can take the Devil long time." He grinned craftily.

I did not hear the village before I arrived. All the

usual sounds of activity had evaporated into the heat. Old Kondea sat on a low stool in his palaver house, garbed only in a bath towel around his hips. He was hunched over a low carving bowl which he held between his bare feet. Braced against the bottom of the bowl was a rice spoon he was carving with his hoelike chisel. Chips flew out on either side. The chisel was a blade of iron attached to the short end of a V-shaped stick. It had belonged to his father before him. The color of the wood was golden brown from the body oil of much handling through many years. It was worn thin at the end from the firm grasp of gnarled hands which had filled the air with the flying chips of many sticks. The tool seemed a part of his own body, an artery through which his soul flowed into the wood he was shaping.

"Moin, Kondea!"

He looked up startled. It took him a moment to come from the world in which he had been living into the one in which I was standing.

"Aye, Moin."

He looked down and saw that he was dressed only in an old towel between his thighs, caught in front and back beneath a raffia string around his hips.

I pointed at a thread of scar on his belly which came above the sagging towel. Kondea burst into a booming laugh. If a drum could laugh it would make such a sound.

Small Boy who stood near to interpret explained, "That place where the American doctor fix the bad belly-humbug that catch the chief. Old Kondea lay in the hospital so." (Small Boy lay on the ground to demonstrate.) "The doctor make the belly to the feet go asleep. Then they cut him open so." (More gestures.) "They forget old Kondea eye no asleep, so the chief, he sit up and look inside his own belly. This make the chief very wise past all chiefs, because no plenty man can say he know the inside of his own belly."

Kondea was still laughing as he disappeared inside his hut. When he came out again he was wearing his flowing blue and white striped country cloth chief-robe and his old black felt American hat. He was then clothed in dignity.

Small Boy brought me a chair and stood by to interpret.

"I come to ask if the chief goes well these days," I said. "I never put eye on him long since, and we fear that a bad thing can catch him."

"The thing that catch the chief is bad for true," Small Boy said. "When a tree is young, people can bring it from the bush and set it down in a new place and it will grow. But when a tree is old and the people move it, it will die. Kondea is old and the plantation people will break his roots and force him to go across the river, and he will die of it. All we sad because we know the chief will die soon."

"But is the body of the chief sick?"

"No, Ma, the body of the chief is strong and same like a young man, as you can see. But a person can die from the heart being sick. It is not so sad to Kondea that he should die as that he cannot be with his fathers who go long time since. You see the old people that are dead and move in the big trees by the village will not know the way to the new town where we must go across the river. You see the rocks there?"

Small Boy indicated the village cromlech, an arrangement of two flat slabs of stone, each laid horizontally on the upright ends of three vertical stones, similar to the dolmens found in Great Britain.

"I see the stones, Small Boy."

"On the day that those stones are brought to the ground our chief will die. And after that all our people who have died in all the time that go before will have no home. And the trees that are their small home, like a palaver house to them, they will all die also so that rubber can grow there."

"How soon must these things be?"

"Well, Ma, the law says that a village cannot be moved while the Devil bush is going on. The chief will keep the girls' school in the bush until he cannot push the plantation more. He say he will finish all the bowls for you before he die. You see the wood in the palaver house?"

There were several hunks of wild-rubber wood in the shed. Latex oozed out of the sides.

"Ask the chief, Small Boy, if it is not necessary to use dry wood for the bowls. The tree-blood runs in these." I could not bear to speak more of Kondea's dying.

Kondea had the look in his eyes of a whipped dog. When Small Boy relayed my question, he brightened, and shook a schoolteacherish forefinger at me.

"The chief says," Small Boy told me, "that he thought he told you long since that when you carve something that is the same thick all over like a bowl, it is good to use the wet wood. Then it dry so it can no lay open in any part. But when you carve a thing like a stick doll that is some places thin and some places fat, then the wood must be dry before you cut the stick."

Kondea sent Small Boy into his house and when he

returned he carried a dozen wooden spoons. They were
wonderfully balanced, with scalloped stems and elliptical
bowls. One of them had a bowl at each end.

"The chief calls that the American spoon," Small Boy
told me. "He says that the American people do everything so quick-time that they need a spoon with two
hands on it. You can use it so." He took the spoon and
showed us how, with a flip of the wrist, food could be
shoveled to the mouth very rapidly. "There is a spoon
to go with each bowl the chief make for you, and five
bowls are already finished."

"Small Boy, tell the chief I like to see him make the
chisel talk to the wood while I watch to learn the way," I
said. I felt that carving would distract him if anything
could. That he would indeed die, I felt sure. I knew of
other natives who had decided they were going to die at
a certain time, even though they seemed to be in perfect
health, and it had always followed that they did die at
that time.

Old Kondea smiled and pride glowed in his eyes. He
extended the chisel toward me.

"The chief say," said Small Boy, "let the tool talk for
your part."

I took the chisel.

"Bring me new stick. I can't spoil your-part work."
The tool was unmanageable in my hands.

"The chief say," said Small Boy, "the country tool,
he not fine like white-man part."

"It not the way the tool be that make it speak," I said.
"It be the talk of the heart to the tool. This country tool,
he hear your part, but he no hear white-man heart."

Kondea nodded and caressed the tool as though it were a live thing.

"The chief say he bring you something."

The something was a large hunk of camwood, the rare purple heartwood that is seldom seen except in slender sticks which are cherished as a source of red-violet dye. I gasped in admiration. Could it be that he was giving me this treasure?

"The chief say this be your part. It no be because chief must dash white man: it be because we two know in the heart how the tool can talk to the wood."

I held the satiny wood to the light and turned it, wondering what I would carve from it.

"What thing you see live inside the stick?" Kondea asked.

I looked at the wood. It shone rich purple.

It must be something regal, I thought, and worthy of the wood!

"Small Boy, tell the chief, the chief-self live inside the stick. Many thing live inside the stick, but the chief speak past all the other. I go make medicine to hold the hand steady that the chief-head can be born out of the wood proper."

Kondea reached out for my right hand and opened the fingers of the upturned palm. Then he laid one of his clever old black hands on mine and showed me that the young white hand and the old black one had the same kind of blisters and callouses.

"When my hand can no more hold the chisel," he told me through Small Boy, "these white hands must talk for the old black one, also."

I could not answer, but I knew that whenever my hands held a chisel, whenever I chose a piece of wood to carve, whenever I sat at the head of our table while my guests ate from the wooden bowls with exquisite wooden spoons, this old man, my guild-brother, would be there with me.

We had stood together, reverent before the surprises in grain revealed in newly carved wood. We had looked at a hunk of wood and seen the countless possibilities of form within its layers. What need had we for the feeble inadequacies of speech? Old man in country-cloth chief-robe and American hat, you of the sensitive hands and shining eyes and booming laugh, had become a vibrant chord in the new song I had slowly learned in this strange land!

The chief's head was never born from the camwood. I decided after a long time that old Kondea lives more vividly within its undisturbed layers.

CHAPTER ELEVEN

The Mask of the Gris-Gris Zo

WILLIE, the son of Chief Kondea, stood in my mud studio, panting for breath with which to speak. He had been running and now he rested by standing storklike on one foot, with the lifted leg akimbo, the sole of the foot pressed against the rigid leg at the knee.

"My pa, the chief, say that you are one of our people now, Ma," Willie told me. "This is the big day the girls come from the Gris-gris bush [the secret school held for adolescent girls, called "Sande" by most of the other tribes]. All our people sit down to see this thing and it is good for you to be there. Today you will pass the lime tree where we stop you the first time you come to see we. I sorry I can no' wait to carry you, but I make the drum talk for the dance and there is much I must do to make ready. Excuse, please, Ma?"

He fidgeted while he spoke and during the courtesy pause afterwards, and with an "I go now," he bounded off through the rubber trees, clearing the fallen logs like an antelope.

When I reached the village, the brother of Kondea was waiting for me by the lime tree. We passed under it and found a narrow path leading through the jungle to a circular clearing about twenty feet in diameter. All the village was seated in half of the circle. The far half was curtained off with a bamboo mat which hung from a top pole like a Venetian blind. Kondea sat on a low chief-chair and there was an empty one beside it for me. The villagers sat cross-legged on the ground. Kondea greeted me in the subdued manner with which people speak at funerals, *sotto voce* and not looking into my eyes. When I was seated, two old women rolled up the mat curtain and secured it to the top pole. At a nod from Kondea, Willie took his place at the large drum on the fringe of the unoccupied half of the circle. Two other men sat at smaller drums. Everyone craned his neck toward the trees back of the circle.

The *Zo*, who is the old and influential woman in charge of the girls during their months or even years in the Gris-gris school, whirled onto the stage when the drums rolled like thunder. She wore a mask, the beauty of which made me gasp. It fitted down over her head and rested on her shoulders. The only break in the cylindrical form was the elaborately carved crested headdress, and the rather small, delicate face. The ears did not extend beyond the cylinder and were small. The back of the head and the neck were scored with straight lines which formed diamond shapes, a shallow curve being scooped out of each diamond. The facial expression was enigmatic; it was both reticent and bold. The eyes were straight slits beneath the arched semicircles of the lids, making them seem slumberous, but the jut of the tapered chin was active and defiant.

When I could stop looking at the mask long enough
to observe the rest of the Zo's costume, I saw that she
wore a long cloak reaching to her knees made of loose
braids of blackened raffia, a pair of men's long trousers
and an old worn-out pair of tennis shoes.

The Zo danced with reserve at first, jerking her torso
in spasmodic movements which she checked before they
were well begun. Then as the restraint dwindled and she
followed through for longer intervals the movements she
had begun, an old woman with a rolled mat swatted at
her smartly. The dance ended in a duel between these

two, the Zo becoming more and more abandoned and the old woman with the mat more and more vicious. Finally the Zo was defeated and fell in a limp heap on the ground, lifting her hands in supplication to the old woman. The old woman helped her to her feet and they walked back to the trees together.

"The meaning of this," Willie told me later, "is that a woman must not let herself go. It is not for a woman to be wild like the leopard in the bush. She must do the one that her man want and not the one her heart tell her. So is the way of a good woman."

"Why did the Zo wear a man's clothing, Willie?" I asked.

"So she does, Ma, because there is something of man in every woman and something of woman in every man. She do so also because in the Gris-gris bush, the Zo teach the girls all the things that man can do to them later so they know all already from the Zo, who take the part of a man to learn them this."

The drums soloed then, without any dancers on the stage. Their beats were vigorous and passionate. I could not follow the pattern because I confused the many off-beats with the emphatic ones. It built up in a slow swell that grew into sustained fiery torment, subsided into contented weariness, and paused. After I had seen the dances which followed I understood it as a sort of overture.

The girls, fifteen of them, were led in by women shaking calabash instruments, made by threading beads and seeds and shells on the strings which cradled the calabash. When the strings were jerked in the rhythm of the drum, the seeds snapped against the gourds. The women wore *lappas* around their hips but their pendulous breasts were unsupported and snapped with the swing of their bodies as the drum played faster and faster. The women made a row at the back of the stage and the girls, fifteen of them, faced the audience in a semicircle. They wore brief raffia skirts and their faces were decorated with white clay. I had not seen the adolescent girls of the tribe before. Their plumpness was in strange contrast to the leanness of the others. Their knees and faces were dimply and a smooth layer of fat covered the rib bones. Later, Willie told me that they had been systematically "fattened" for three months before their coming out, and that this was a severe drain on the rice stores of the tribe. I guessed their ages to range from eight to fourteen, although I could not be sure of this. The faces of all of them and the bodies of all except the taller ones seemed childlike and undeveloped.

Each girl danced alone before they all danced in a group. The dance was to demonstrate what each had learned in the Gris-gris school about the ways of pleasing men. There was nothing coarse nor vulgar about this display. The frankness absorbed what under other circumstances might have been lascivious. They were very serious; there was no snickering nor giggling, no attempt to be "precious" or coy.

I wished for a time that I had been able to record the nimble beauty of their movements with a moving-picture camera. Then I realized that in any setting but this, and without understanding of the reason for the display, it would be misinterpreted. I think the dances seemed beautiful rather than crass burlesque because they were done with intense sincerity and because there was no attempt to augment them with tinsel or luxury, nothing comparable to filmy veils and rhinestone patches. There was only the prolific jungle for backdrop, and the clay of the fruitful earth for body decoration. They were demonstrating to their people, and to the watching men who might buy them, that they had learned well the serious business of being women. They were lithe saplings of the forest swayed by the trapped air of the hollow drums, and they danced as though the drum thuds were but an echo of the pounding of their own hearts, a spilling out into movement of vitality. There was something aristocratic about them, as though they were conscious of the as yet unbestowed wealth of their bodies, which in a few months would become child-swollen and begin to break.

Although each girl portrayed the same ideas in her dance, no two danced alike. Some of them ended in an ecstatic body-twitching which left the girl in a trance on the ground with her face set rigid as death. Others cut their dance short in the height of its fiery, exultant movement. Some of them never reached this frenzied pitch of movement but danced languidly with a sort of desolate yearning in their faces and finished their dance by slowly extending their palms to the sky as if in supplication.

The Bassaus do not declitorize their girls in the Grisgris bush, as is the custom of many of the other tribes, who believe that this ceremony is as important for the girls as circumcision for their boys. The interior tribesmen

say that it is this neglect of the Bassaus which causes a
Bassau woman to be "frisky too much and care what man
buy her," thus causing much trouble to her parents in
arranging bride-price, and in selecting a husband.

The girls seemed unaware of any of the audience as
individuals. If they had any preference for particular
men this was not the time when they showed it.

When all of them had danced separately, they formed
a circle and danced together while the shake-shakes and
drums reached new crescendos. Willie's corneous fingers
moved so rapidly over the drum they made streaks like a
flicked whip. The Zo stood in the center of the circle
and girls swayed past her. When the dance was over the
old woman with the mat brought water and girls washed
the clay decorations from their faces in the big common
calabash. After they had disappeared into the jungle
they re-appeared wearing lappas of new country cloth.
They had now "taken cloth" and after the prescribed
period of a month, they might be bought for wives. They
would bring about forty-eight dollars each, the market
price at that time for a cow, but the money could be paid
in installments whereas cash was usually demanded for a
cow.

All during the performance Kondea sat with his chin
on his chest, sunk in melancholia, seeming to see nothing
though his eyes were open. It was like a pageant of birth
and death. It seemed to me that he was dying even as
these children, whose breasts were scarcely swollen, were
being born into women.

When the ceremony was over and the feast-rice and

goats were cooking over fires, I asked Kondea if I might see the mask the Zo had worn. He hesitated at first and then sent for it.

"Did you carve this, Kondea?"

"Aye, Ma."

Not even the talk of carving could rouse him from his apathy.

"I think that this is the best work I have seen from your hand, Chief. Willie, tell the chief the thing I say."

Kondea nodded but made no answer.

Willie escorted me home. There was a large bulge under his small-chief's robe, which he screened by a length of country cloth. When we were outside the village a safe distance, Willie showed me that he was carrying the Zo mask.

"The chief say," said Willie, "that because you think this is the best thing he make, he want you to carry it. Some small mistake stay for all the thing he make for you. When he cut this one, he sit long time in the jungle and the hand of the old carvers who die long since come and hold his hand steady so there is no mistake in any part of it. It may be the people of the village vex small if they know it go from our medicine house, so I carry it under my coat."

"What will the Zo do for a mask the time you are chief, Willie?" I spoke as though Kondea had already died.

"Ma, I will go in the bush and sit a long time and pray that the old man who held the arm of Kondea can find the way to come to the new place to help me in this, and in all that I do, to have sense. When Kondea show me how to cut the hairpins that I give you first time I came to your house, when he show me how to carve the rice bowls and the spoons, the reason for all this take-care in showing me these things is so I can carve a mask like this one when the time comes for me to do it. All that he show me is path to this that I have yet to do. An old chief can die and a young chief take his work, but all the time, all the years, small girls grow to be woman, and it be the woman, not the chief, that keeps the tribe alive. That is the reason there must be much take-care in the mask for the Gris-gris Zo."

The woman Zo finally finished her rites with the adolescent girls in the sacred grove; the law could not be held off any longer. The stone slabs of the cromlech were knocked to the ground, and soldiers demolished the huts.

Soon after the festivities were over, Old Kondea went to his people whose spirits whisper in the leaves of the jungle ceiling above the stone altar of the Spirit Tree. He died quietly in his palaver house, sitting on the low chief-stool, with the chisel still in his hand.

CHAPTER TWELVE

Quay-Quay and Sahda

I HAD little taste for carving wood after Kondea was gone. He had become so large a part of all I did with chisels and mallet, the work was empty without him.

I turned to clay for a less exacting medium. Quay-Quay, a Mano man in the Research Camp, had told me of a special kind which "never break in the fire." This clay came from a sacred swamp near Ganta and could be taken away only by certain old Mano women who knew how to pray to it.

Quay-Quay was willing to walk with two other Mano boys across Liberia to the boundary of French Guinea to get this special prayed-to clay. They came back, each carrying a five-gallon kerosene tin full of it on his head.

When I went to the Camp to get it, I saw the stick doll.

She stood in the piazza of Quay-Quay's hut, a carved female figure about two feet high, made from one stick of cottonwood blackened with the juices of the special plant which are used only to dye masks and fetishes. On top of her head was a coronal disk which held a Bible! Her only clothing was a swag of stained country cloth, pulled askew to reveal the crotch, garishly limned with red lead, enhancing her awe and power by rendering her permanently menstruous.

"We pray to her to give us pickin," Quay-Quay explained.

The figure was the reality of woman, condensed in wood, an intensification of all that is female. Her breasts were tapered cylinders which protruded at right angles from the torso. A natural split in the wood revealing the milk-white fiber beneath the skin-deep stain seemed the revolt of turgid glands. The arms and legs were almost-cylinders with two perfect circles to mark kneecaps. The head was delicate and small, in strange contrast to the hoydenish body.

Intuitively, I approved of the stick doll as good sculpture. It succeeded well in what many sculptors who make a cult of "modernism" almost succeed in doing. There was a concept of body planes and structures and volumes without distracting fidelity to variations from basic shapes. When I looked at it, I felt infected with its implications, as though the emotions of the carver were readily contagious. I had "caught" them by looking and running my fingertips over his work. I believe this conviction that here was good sculpture would come readily to anyone, whether he had ever studied art or not, unless he were so prejudiced with the idea that art must be "realistic" that he could not pass over this barrier. The carver had not "manipulated nature" nor tried to interpret it; he had let nature manipulate him. The surging desire to be fertile and to perpetuate himself had excited him to the action of carving this intense femaleness.

Without ever having heard of Dewey's concept of art as "experience consciously transformed" and without knowing that what he was doing was art, he had modified it into experience almost unconsciously transformed.

As I looked at the figure and thought of the way a similar fetish had changed the whole course of contemporary painting and sculpture, it seemed to me that many artists whose work I had seen had put the cart before the horse. Some of them deliberately distort to achieve a "primitive" effect and the result is a travesty. When a subject is *felt* with all its basic geometrics and stresses of structure, stripped of concealing detail, and what is deeply felt is honestly portrayed, these felt emphases will "distort" the result. This is a different matter from starting out with intended murder of apparent reality. And I do not think that these distortions will appear similar to those in the work of a native African carver because no one who is not saturated with their beliefs and reactions will "feel" toward anything exactly the way jungle men will feel toward it.

"How is it, Quay-Quay," I said, "that you have here on your house both the Bible and the god of your people? Is it not true that you must believe in one and refuse the other? Can any man give his heart to two gods?"

Quay-Quay scratched himself in a long sweep beginning at the groin and ending, without pause en route, in the hollow under his arm. This is a nervous gesture which chimpanzees as well as natives use when trying to resolve a confusion. Finally the slender fingers twisted the moist hair of his armpit calmly and he spoke:

"I think, Ma, that it is not two gods, but all one. Your people say that God lives in the big book. The Mandingos say that Truth lives in the big book, but not God self. They say that the Jesus in your book was a great man with plenty sense, but he only a small boy beside their true prophet. Our own fathers say that God lives in the big bush, in the high hills, in the animals, in the stones, in the trees, in every branch and leaf and small stick of the trees, and that he speaks to we through our people that have died. If one people is right altogether, then the others are altogether wrong, and we know that this is not true. We have heard the talk of our dead fathers in our hearts, and we have heard God talk softly-softly in the trees. We have seen the strong medicine of the Mandingos. One sits down in this town now and makes medicine for we, so I can get pickin. We have seen also the strong medicine of your people. My town is not far from Ganta, and for many years Doctor Harley has filled his needles and made strong medicine for we.

"So it must be that there is some of true in all and some of not-true in all. *And what is true is all one!* So I

think that the idol and the Book of your people and the
sense of the Mandingo can all live for my hut at the
same time."

An idol raising the Bible above the steaming excrement of dogs and fowls while this Spinoza of the forest
scratched himself, and tried to make me understand what
he believed.

"Quay-Quay," I said, "I think that I hear the thing
that you say. And now I want to tell you this: When I

first saw this wooden god, I wanted it because the way it
is cut from the wood is very fine. The people in my
country who cut stick can like it too much because this
way of cutting person from stick is ma to the way we-part
try this time. One big man carry one figure cut same
way from wood from your country down the coast, to a
big town in the land of the French people, a place called
Paris. When the other people who cut stick and paint on
cloth see it, they see it is fine past their old way because
it talks more loud to the heart. Now they try this native
way, but for the most part, they do' know how. Myself,
I come to learn this way. That is the reason I want to
carry, first time, this that I see on your piazza. But now,
I see that for you it is necessary, and I cannot ask it from
your hand. For I see that the Bible can be trampled in
the dirt in this country without it be resting on the head
of the god of your fathers."

"Ma, you know that I can read small," Quay-Quay
said. "I sit by the fire in the night-time and put my eye
on the thing it say in your Book. Then I take pencil and
I mark the thing that talk the same way as the old men
of my people. I find plenty thing that be the same. How
is it that your people think they bring to we that which
we have already?"

"Like what thing, Quay-Quay?"

"In the Mission, Ma, where I learn to read small, they
tell we it is good to give something that belong to we to
some one who has not got this thing. This has been the
way of our people for all time. When I get rice, I give
part to any Mano man that ask me, and sometimes I
would even give small to a Gio man, but not to a Bassau,

for they are lazy and because they are lazy they are not my brother. When I stay to the Mission I do steward-boy work for the missionary and he give me white singlet because he no like me to stand before him without clothes. It is a fine singlet. One Mano boy see it and he like it too much so I give it to him because myself I like the sun on my skin. Then the missionary vex! Oh, how he vex! But the thing I do be the very thing he tell me first time that be good to do. I ask him how it is that he can tell we that it good to give unto the poor and then he vex when I do it."

I took the Bible which sagged limply over the edge of my palms. The book was rotten with mold and had traces of smoke and water like books at a fire sale. The cockroaches had devoured most of the imitation-leather cover and the glue on the back. Many of the pages were stuck together and crumbled in pieces when they were separated. The paper had absorbed all of the odors that waft to the loft of a hut. There were many marked passages, smirched with soft lead and the greasy trail of a laboriously tracing forefinger.

"Talk it out loud to me, Ma. The writing lets loose into talk easy for you. With me, the meaning of one word gets lost before I find the one that follow. And the meanings of many words are things I do not know at all."

"But the people wait for their rice, Quay-Quay."

"Let the people wait, Ma. I have been waiting longer for new meanings."

"All right, Quay-Quay. I will sit down in the village while my husband goes to the other divisions."

We sat in the concavity of the worn doorstep with the

idol beside us, leaning forward on her flat feet in the posture of listening, now that the weight of the book was lifted from her head. The people in the camp gathered around and listened for a time, and then tiring of words they could not understand, they sprawled out in the sun and slept or gathered around their carved *wari* boards, playing the game with silent concentration.

The Bible fell open to the twentieth chapter of Exodus, and I read what Quay-Quay had underlined:

> "An altar of earth thou shalt make unto me, and shall sacrifice thereon thy burnt offerings, and thy peace offerings, thy sheep . . . and if thou wilt make me an altar of stone, thou shalt not build it of hewn stone; for if thou lift up thy tool upon it, thou hast polluted it. Neither shall thou go up by steps unto the altar, that thy nakedness be not discovered thereon."

"You see, Ma," said Quay-Quay, "that is the one we part do. We carry the big stone to the cotton tree. We never put chisel to the stone; we leff it the way God make it. Then we carry earth there, the one the ants build up straight with the head on top, same like a man-stick. Then we put the sacrifice there. We no got plenty sheep, and God knows that one. But we take white rice and white chicken and make the sacrifice. And the woman who goes there to pray for pickin wears lappa; she can't go naked. We know plenty Bible palaver without we know it be from the Bible!"

Much of the Psalms were underlined. Quay-Quay asked me to reread several times, "Who walketh on the wings of the wind."

"The Book say," he pointed out, "that God is in the

wind. He must be same way in the water and the stones
and the trees, and that is the one our fathers believe.
These words have the sound of the wind when he talk
softly-softly in the trees. Say the words again, Ma."

"Who walketh on the wings of the wind." I liked the
sound of it, too.

We read through the Old Testament taboos and Quay-
Quay explained to me that he did not think the Book
meant to say that all people should have the same taboos
because each tribe and even different clans within a tribe
have different taboos. Monkey and snake were taboo to
him and he did not consider these as restricting as the
taboos imposed on the tribes of Israel.

"And now, Ma," said Quay-Quay, "I like you to read
me the story of Joseph. Myself, I read that story many
times, but it walks slow when I read it. I tell the story to
the Mandingo who sits here to make medicine, and he
knows the story also. That man, he vex like hell-o when
he learn that the Christians call it a story from the Bible.
He say it be a story from the Mohammedan book. Wait
small, I show you something."

Quay-Quay scuttled into his house and spoke in French
to the sleeping Mandingo medicine man. He reappeared
with a roll of paper under his arm and the scowling Mandingo at his heels.

"Look, Ma," said Quay-Quay, and he unrolled the
paper.

The paper was a garish color print of an Egyptian
courtyard. Against an opulent background which might
have been the palace of Queen Nefertiti, Potiphar's

voluptuous wife was halted midway in a strip-tease, with one bulbous scarlet-tipped breast thrust at the bland face of an unsmiling Joseph, while Potiphar skulked in the background between vigorous stems of papyrus.

"I wish to buy this to show to my people," I said to the wrathy Mandingo.

"*Abas!*" he fairly shouted, and snatching his print, he shuffled into the house so fast he lost one of his heelless sandals, shaking his flowing robes as he walked, like a wet dog. Later I was able to buy a duplicate of the print on the boundary of French Guinea.

"Now, Ma," said Quay-Quay, "the meaning of all this to me is that it is all one. You see just now how the God-book and the Allah-book talk the same thing. And you see how the God-book and the talk of my people is the same. So God is all one."

"I do see, Quay-Quay. Some people who think they have much sense do not know this true thing. These people look for the way it is different and they set the eye so hard that they cannot see the way it is the same."

"Ma," he said, "can it be that you will find it in your heart to come again and do this thing that we do this afternoon?"

"I will come again," I said. "And I have a book that I can give into your hand. It has in it the meaning of many English words, and sometimes, small photo to show the look of things. Each word lives with the other words that begin with the same letter. When you read of a unicorn, you will look in the 'U' part of the book and you will see a unicorn is same like a horse, only a horn like your snuff horn grows for the top of the head."

"It must be a very great book," he said. "My heart will lie down for that one."

We said no more about the idol, but on the next rice-issue day when my husband carried the dictionary to Quay-Quay, he came back in the evening with the idol under his arm. There was a note written in thick pencil on a piece of pasteboard tied around its neck. It read:

Dear Ma Warner,

Thank you, yah, for the fine book. Already I read to *Abaris*. Tonight when work finish I can tell my people about the medicine man in the Appolo tribe who don't take chop and who sit down on his hunting arrow and fly like a bird. I don't think Qua Qwoi can do that one. Maybe he can try and all the people in the camp can laugh when he fall down. I will learn much sense before I finish read this fine book. I will read all.

Your obedient servant,

Quay-Quay

Postscriptum. The time when you leave, the stick doll fall off her feet and lie down on her face in the dirt. I think the meaning of this is that she want to live for your house because the same is the way a small child can do when he vex to go with person.

Postscriptum 2. I don't think I can make a pickin with this stick doll anyhow, so do not think my shame of having no child is upon you because you keep her. The Mandingo medicine man makes me some medicine with black cola and I think that will bring me luck in the matter of my craving. If no good, than I can pray to the Bible."

Quay-Quay's woman was a beautiful Vai girl who had learned to speak English at the Episcopal mission school at Cape Mount. She helped Quay-Quay read the Bible and the dictionary and tried to teach me a bit of Vai script. The Vai are the only tribe who have made symbols for the sounds of their speech. Their "country book" is beautiful design, but difficult to comprehend.

It was pleasant to sit with Sahda in her hut. She kept her house well. The floor was brush-swept, the fire well tended, the cooking pots sand-scoured. The one ornament was a wind chime which tinkled obbligato as she told me charming Vai folktales and taught me to spin the native cotton.

She had made the ornament by plaiting palm leaves
into a fan which she fastened to the end of a wire. The
wire was threaded through a green glass bottle from
which the bottom had been removed. The fan caught the
breeze and tinkled the wire against the glass. The sound
had a gay treble-laughter quality. It was similar to that
made by the glass fragments strung on a red silk cord
which my grandmother kept in her hallway, a sound
which belongs with shadowy coolness.

The Vai women are noted for their beauty, but the
loveliness of Sahda was something beyond facial contour
or tribal characteristics. She was intelligent and imagina-
tive and these qualities shone in her face. After Quay-
Quay brought me the prayed-to clay, carrying it the
depth of the country on his head, I knew I must use it to
model Sahda. This was difficult to arrange because of her
shyness. When I told her that she was beautiful and that
I wanted to keep her beauty by catching it in clay, there
was no joy in her face.

"No woman is beautiful who has not borne a child,"
she said, and bowed her head.

Sahda sat for me finally, perhaps because Quay-Quay
wished it. After the first trying morning when her em-
barrassment was painful, we had fine times together. Her
fund of stories in which the animals spoke great truths
and behaved like humans, wise and foolish, was inex-
haustible.

One morning, Sahda brought me a wind chime like
the one which hung under her own eaves. The fibers
were pinched where they intersected, and relaxed into
broad flatness between crossings. All were held in shape

by the meticulously braided strands which framed it. I was intrigued by its ingenuity and colors and textures and sound. But I was enchanted also with its movement in the way that I am fascinated by a Calder mobile in the Museum of Modern Art.

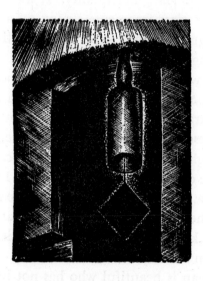

She sat before my fireplace on a low stool. The sibilant flames threw copper lights and purple shadows on her smooth bronze skin. The breeze, whipping wetness before it, whistled in the mud chimney, and agitated the traveler's palm with a strange rustling that was like an unknown language. It plucked at the edge of thatch along the roof, and slapped at the palm fan on the end of the wind chimes.

"That thing I bring you is a small something so the breeze can make play," Sahda said. "The breeze is a small boy and this his doll."

I added clay to the lids of the head, trying to get the elusive swell that is not a puffiness but a ripe fullness above her large eyes. Sahda did not watch me. Her eyes were on me but not seeing me, straining beyond to see as well as hear the dallying of currents of air with trees and shrubs and grass.

"You hear the wind?" Sahda asked me finally.

"Yes, Sahda, I hear."

"It is my radio!"

Her eyes glowed and widened, her lips parted, and she held her breath to catch every nuance of the wind's song.

I told Sahda that I heard, but that was not really true. The language of the travelers' palm was not secret to her. I was excluded because I had not listened long nor quietly enough. Sahda felt a cadence of the elements running through her being, with tones of depth and height which were beyond the range of my sensibility. I could not hear all that Sahda heard nor feel all that she felt because I had not earned that right by living closely with the weather. Since she was a child tied on her mother's back, the wind had been her song, the night had been her inner silence and loneliness, the storms wresting the jungle had been her unleashed strivings. For this, Sahda, I would gladly barter my radio. You say I come from a land of "boxes that talk" but I am humble before you whose soul is not choked with static. You sat in front of your hut and plaited this toy for the wind child and brought it here that he might bless my yard by playing with it. But the thing I would have from you is your ability to put the wind's song into the melody of living.

CHAPTER THIRTEEN

The Twisted Iron Money

Knowing my joy in a well-told tale, Sahda invited me to a "talk-palaver" in the camp.

A large group of natives squatted around a low fire, taking turns at tall stories.

Shouts of "Bwaho! Bwaho!" from the crowd broke into and followed each story. The louder the "Bwahos," the more incredible, and therefore the more virtue in the tale that was being told.

I had hoped that Sahda would participate because she was the best storyteller I had heard.

"No, Missy," she said. "My talk is beside my own fire; it is not for all to hear."

Among the contestants was Kutaboo, steward boy in the house of one of our friends.

Kutaboo had a large reputation for his imagination, and everyone sat forward-bent to hear. That he had been allowed to speak last indicated that his was expected to be the best story of all. He regarded a piece of twisted iron money (worth half a farthing), dug his scalp with it, twirled it like a baton, and jabbed it toward the audience as he spoke. I understood from the gestures that the tale had to do with strength and with eating. For the latter Kutaboo's reputation was also large. He was tolerated in the household where he worked simply because he was comic. He cooked poorly and cleaned seldom. It was a saying among the scornful Bassau servants at my house that the Gbonde boy of our friend's house grew fatter and fatter, while his master grew every day more slender, and were it not that the master sat often at our table and ate good Bassau cooking, he would surely be already dead.

The "Bwahos" that interrupted Kutaboo's tale, and the laughter, often drowned out his voice. During these enforced pauses for order, he cupped his several chins in a cherubic palm and glared in most uncherubic superiority at the other storytellers. This, too, the audience liked and applauded.

I was eager to hear Kutaboo's story in English and it was with that in mind that we stopped at our friend's house the next day.

We sat in undusted chairs in the living room and drank tepid water which Kutaboo swore he had remembered to boil even though he had forgotten to fill the trays for ice cubes in the refrigerator, which did not work anyway because he had forgotten to put kerosene in the lamp under the ice machine, and since there was no kerosene to cook the ice, why fill the pans with water?

"This better be a good story or it's the sack for you, this time, for true," his master said.

"Yeah, boss," Kutaboo answered with mock sadness.

He had forgotten his duties before and the threat of the sack was only a gesture; well he knew it, but it was respectful to look sad.

He stood in the center of the room and engaged all of our eyes before he would begin. I, who was expected to coerce good housewifery among the servants of our bachelor friends, rubbed a little dust off the chair arm with my forefinger and looked at Kutaboo reproachfully. He met the severity of my eyes and brushed it aside with a shifting of his own attention to the faces of the men. I was bothering, womanlike, with inconsequential matters when I was about to hear a fine thing. All right, he would ignore me for a while and talk as a man to men, who knew what really was important in this world.

"This is the story I tell the people." He gave a puckish grin.

"My name is Kutaboo. All the people know this but it is proper for a man to look at people and say his name. I be one half Gbonde, and one half German, and one half United States.

"Sometimes I say I be one half Akron, but it is no difference, because I think Akron is another name for the United States, though some people, who do not know, say that Akron is not as large as the whole United States but only one village. And this is how it is that I am one half of each of these: I be one half Gbonde for my mother is Gbonde. I be one half German because my pa be a German trader that go to the interior to look for gold. The chief look on him and see that he is fine and give him for wife for the night, my ma, because she is fine past all the girls in the town. Also, I one half United

States because I come for Firestone and learn my man-ways on the plantation.

"So soon as I am born, I jump up like so [springing on bandy legs] from the mat where my ma lay, and I vex for chop. I look on my ma and I see that I hurt her plenty because I be big already like I see three rice-plantings before I leave her. I hungry for chop but I more sorry for my ma because I hurt her, so I run like deer to the river and bring cold water and Cola, for she tire and hot with the much work she do to make me leave her.

"When I come back, the people give me rice but I can no' like rice so I vex for strong chop. The people say, 'All right, let us give him irons [the twisted money]. I bite one iron in two and I vex because he no be hot. So the people put the iron in the fire until he red like a Mandingo hat. That one I eat, I eat, I eat, until the ma's pa, who is the chief, is a poor man. I tell him, 'No mind, old Pa, because I can make plenty more again for you.'

"Then I go to the iron hill. It is the walk of a strong man in two days but I go there like so [one big step]. I take the rock in my hand and squeeze it same like a lime. The stone gets hot from my squeezing and the iron runs out like water. Then I catch the iron when it runs proper thin like a small river, and I put one end in my teeth and I twist the iron and it turns like a raffia string that the country people rub against their legs. Then I put him in my teeth, for I born with teeth already big, and bite each piece off the proper length for money. I step on the end and it lays flat like a blacksmith had hit it with a hammer, and it is proper money.

"After, I carry to the chief but the money is too plenty to stay for my arms so I pick up a piece of the river. I break it off like paper and the length of it is same like a day's walk on the bank. I make this into a sack for the iron and the way I sew it is with needle I get when I reach for the lightning and break off some that has a sharp point. For thread I take big black snakes. To make the eye in the needle I spit through the lightning, so [he sent a piercing stream through the window screen]. After, I want to go to my people the short way but no path through the bush, so I put plenty breath in my face and hold my belly tight and blow. The trees fall down but they no fall across the path. They lay so [he parted his hair with a country comb to show the manner in which the path was clear]. One tree when it fall kill a bush cow, so I put the river full of irons on my back and the bush cow on my head and lay all before the chief. He glad and he say that he think it will be that when I grow to be a man I will be rather strong. From that day until I come to the plantation I never take no chop but hot irons. Now I am very civilized and I like tin better than iron, and when the master gives me some fine American chop I eat it whole and long after when my belly has finished with the tin I know the taste of the small corn-beef inside.

"But I am very sad this time because now my pa is dead because of the white man's tribal war. My pa sit down in the big tribe of Germany and his heart hungry to put eye on the small pickin he made. So he go outside his hut and take a big banana leaf, and he climb a high mountain where he can look down on all the world. And he set his face in all ways and see that it is all good and he want to have it all for his tribe. But he say, 'I will leff that for now and go first to the land of the Gbondies to see my son.' So he get on the banana leaf and jump off the big hill and fly and fly. And the French people see him and think he is an airplane and they shoot him so he fall down. He fly very high and on the path to the ground he catch hold small-time on the back of an eagle, and he tell the eagle, 'Go for the plantation and tell my son that I die because of the war. The war cannot allow person to go to see his own people; it is for this stupid thing that I die.'

"Yesterday-time the eagle come to me and tell me this thing and I not glad. Now this same eagle lives for the house of Boss Burgess, and if my master agree-o, I will go there this day and see my friend Kessilie who is steward to Mr. Burgess and talk more with the eagle. You agree, Boss? I can walk strong and come back soon-morning to cook you fine breakfast."

"Your name should be John Henry," I said.

He tried to pull in his squabby stomach to make himself taller, and said with affronted dignity, "My name is Kutaboo."

Then he searched the big pocket over his heart, a patch pocket sewed in horizontal stripes over the vertical stripes of his knee-length chief-robe, and pulled out a twisted iron. He made a sort of bow by spreading apart his fat knees and dipping his buttocks and handed the iron to me.

"I dash you this iron, Ma. You can no buy plenty thing with him. The Akron money is good past this for

buy things." (He looked appreciatively at my purse.)
"But when you go again to your people and you sit down
in your palaver house, and your heart no lie down because maybe he hungry sometimes for this place, you
take this iron in your hand and you can feel the sun hot
on the iron mountain and you will be strong."

I took the iron in my hand. Kutaboo waited with dignity while I fished a sixpence out of my purse. He
dropped it in the big pocket from which he had taken
the iron.

"My heart be civilized, too, same like my stomach,"
said Kutaboo. "He like the talk of silver past the way
he like the talk of iron. I put the silver here and he talk
to my glad heart all the time I walk to the house of my
friend Kessilie." He glanced at his master to see if his
trip would be vetoed, and seeing that it was not, he
wobbled out of the room, and across the lawn, where he
disappeared into the rubber trees in the direction of the
house of Planter Burgess who collected eagles.

CHAPTER FOURTEEN

A Mano Goes to His People

H AD IT NOT BEEN for Quay-Quay's persistent efforts to father a child, I would not have learned about the lost wax.

Quay-Quay was somewhat handicapped in his project by being "civilized." The old tribal laws would have offered several helpful solutions. Had he suspected that the fault lay in himself, he might have asked a close friend to stay with Sahda until the goal was achieved. Failing success, he would have sent Sahda back to her people, demanded a return of the bride-price, and bought himself a new woman with the money.

Even if Quay-Quay's education had not precluded these alternatives, I think he would have kept Sahda. They seemed genuinely in love. The fact that they could both read a little and enjoyed reading together was a strong bond. They both had intellectual curiosity and fine imaginations. The only flaw in their life together was her barrenness. When the black cola which is considered to have powerful fertilizing qualities was of no help, Quay-Quay took to collecting brass.

Brass bars were part of the miscellaneous cargo with

which the American Liberians bartered for their first strip of Liberian land, and brass has entered the country as trade goods ever since. Whenever Quay-Quay could get some, ancient or modern, he did so. Old bracelets, small bits from junked automobiles, knife handles, nothing was too small or large for him to collect. After work he sat on his porch and laboriously scraped it into small shavings.

This went on for weeks, during which he was reluctant to discuss the reason for his mysterious labor. It was by accident that I stumbled on the answer.

At a forest forge near the native village of Jacobtown was a fine blacksmith who could make needles for my Singer sewing machine. I walked there to talk about having some new ones made, and was surprised to find Quay-Quay sitting beside the bellows, watching the smith. On the floor of the palaver house were open bags containing the brass scrapings.

They did not hear my approach and after they saw me they had no time to cover the object on the mat between them. It was a wax figure about six inches high, of a frighteningly virile man. It had been painstakingly modeled in wild bees' wax. The smith was having trouble with the most conspicuous extremity, which kept breaking off. Quay-Quay interpreted this repeated casualty as a bad omen and looked despondent.

A native forge is taboo to a woman. Moreover, it is a sacred place where hunted men can take refuge, as they did in the medieval cathedrals. I had been above the law at this one, perhaps because I worked with chisels. The smith had even shown me how to temper steel by heat-

ing it to the proper color and then plunging it into palm
oil. But I knew that this day I would not be welcome. I
was standing where I had no right to be and I had seen
a sacred thing which I had no right to see. The only
decent thing to do was to leave quietly, much as I wanted
to stay.

As I wheeled reluctantly, Quay-Quay turned and saw
me. He made a quick gesture to cover the figure with a
corner of the smith's spread robe, then realizing that I
had already seen it, his hand fell to his side.

Why he asked me to stay, I don't know. It may be that
he felt my sculpture could give me a sympathetic understanding of the wax image. He already knew that I was
sympathetic with his and Sahda's problem.

I sat on the mat and watched.

The smith brushed the figure with wet clay. As soon as this first clay layer had dried, another was added, then another, until the wax was a core in a thick lump of mud. An opening was left from one of the figure's feet to the outside of the clay. Another smaller opening was made from the head to the exterior of the mud mold.

Quay-Quay worked the bellows. They were pouches of monkey skin attached to a hollow mound of clay. By punching one skin and then the other, air was forced through the mound of clay and out a small opening on the opposite side where charcoal burned. Thus were the brass shavings melted after long exertion at the bellows.

When the brass was molten, it was carefully poured into the opening in the foot end of the mold. As the wax melted, it ran out the head end, the metal taking its place in the mold.

"The wax, he lost proper, now," the smith said, as a fine thread of metal trickled out the head end.

When the brass had cooled and the clay was removed, the little fertility god was technically perfect. The bump of its head where the brass had trickled down the vent left for the melted wax was filed away. It was ready for whatever use Quay-Quay could make of it.

The lost-wax process was not lost. Here was the *cire-perdue* process used by Greek sculptors four hundred years before Christ. How did the technique find its way into the Liberian forests? The answer may lie in the Benin bronzes. (Some authorities believe that the Portuguese brought a knowledge of *cire-perdue* to Benin.)

Here in the jungle where so few things survive for any length of time, an old art still lived.

"How do you know this thing you do?" I asked the smith.

"I have it from my pa who has long since gone to the old ones," he said. "The words of the old ones," he said, "are same like the sky. No man walks to the end."

I admired the figure with Quay-Quay whose spirit was revived by the perfection of the casting. The idol's facial expression was exceedingly grim.

"How is it," I said, "that the man looks so in his face?"

He quoted a pungent tribal proverb, the gist of which was that laughter is no asset to a man undertaking the matter which had become the obsession of his life.

Quay-Quay and Sahda had their own version of a piggy bank. They dug a hole about three feet deep in the center of their hut. At the bottom they placed a large clay country pot with a lid. They chipped a hole out of the lid just large enough to admit the end of a length of gas pipe. Then, with concrete, they encased the pot and pipe. When the earth was replaced in the hole, the upper end of the pipe was flush with the floor. More concrete was placed around that.

Each pay day, several shillings were dropped down the pipe to rest in the pot below. Every time Sahda marketed a few chickens or some of the sesame seeds she grew, the money went down the pipe. They kept no record of their savings.

"When the pot is full and the pipe stands full, and will eat no more silver, I will know it is sufficient," Quay-Quay explained.

"Sufficient for what?" I asked.

"Sufficient for me to look my people in the face," he said. "When the rice boils for a man home from the plantation, it boils for white money. My pa is old now. He is the Chief of Buapwa. Small time remain before my people call me to be the new chief. I cannot go with empty hands. Against that day, I feed money to the pot."

When I went to their hut one day, and found Quay-Quay excavating his floor with a pick, I thought the long-expected news had arrived.

"Your father, the chief, Quay-Quay? Is it that he has gone to be with the old ones [died]?"

There was no grief in the beaming face Quay-Quay lifted above the pick.

"Oh, no, Ma! That is not the something I have to tell you. The something is this — *Sahda is making a pickin!*

Soon-morning, today, she tell me. Now I take the silver,
we go for Buapwa. I will brush farm and build house
and learn chief-ways. It may be my pa will live to see my
son! Sahda must not walk the trail past next moon, so we
go soon-time. The belly of the pot and the belly of Sahda
be full. We don't go empty."

"Where is Sahda now?" I wanted to congratulate her,
too, and to see how she reacted to the great news.

"Sahda walks alone in the big bush, Ma. A woman
when she is making pickin takes on strange ways," he said
with husbandly understanding.

Before they left, Quay-Quay gave me the brass god I
had seen him and the blacksmith making.

"I don't need that one now, Ma," he said happily.

I wanted them to stay so that Sahda's baby could be
delivered at the Firestone Hospital. She was delicate and
finely made, and I shuddered to think of her suffering
the rude and unclean ministrations of the old Mano
women when her time came. The natives believe that no
man should come in the house where there is a woman
in labor, even though the man is a doctor.

"A Mano pickin should be born in Mano Country,"
Quay-Quay insisted stubbornly. "No mind, Ma, the
pickin will come good."

"But," I argued, "Sahda is Vai, even though you are
Mano. You are both civilized. You belong to the new
kind of Liberia that this country needs. You do not belong to just one tribe."

"I am a Mano, Ma," he said proudly.

After they left, I did not see them for five months.
Sahda sent me several tatua-books (notes carried from

town to town by messengers) to say that she was well, that Quay-Quay was making farm, that soon they would have a new house of their own, that her heart was hungry for me, and that I must sit down with them when I came to the interior.

I walked to Buapwa in time to see the building of Quay-Quay's new house. Sahda was radiant and even more beautiful than before her pregnancy. She cooked my rice herself, and sat long hours with me in the hut the old chief assigned for my use.

We walked in the jungle and she taught me native plants, and their uses, the wood stains, the fish poisons, the medicinal herbs. At night, we sat on the piazza and told stories. Her tales were more of the wonderful Vai folklore. The ones she wanted from me were Old Testament stories. Now that she was expecting a baby she had special sympathy for Hannah because "the Eternal had shut up her womb; and this went on year after year."

"Aye, I know that one," she said, "and the taunts also. But no more," and she glanced proudly at the swell below her lappa. The prayer that Hannah sang, with its "the barren woman has seven children," Sahda took for prophecy. She too would bear seven children! And this first one they would name Samuel.

As we made good talk, night after night, the moon grew full. It exaggerated everything it touched with its light. The roofs of the village houses were furbished silver, and vast like great candle snuffers, all but extinguishing the shadowed walls beneath.

I had admired the mud structures I had seen on the old plantation, but it was not until I had lived in Buapwa and had seen the jungle and river with Sahda's eyes that I realized the noble beauty of native houses. One has to see them in the changing atmosphere, which is like a matrix, holding in it the houses, and the jungle surrounding them and the river sliding past.

In the dimness before sunrise, the Moslem muezzin calls the Mohammedans of the village to prayer. The call is a long, coaxing thread of sound, slim and strong enough to pull the sun above the treetops. People pour out of the houses, sleepwalking to the waterside to douse themselves awake in the cold stream.

The river in the early morning is sleep-sluggish like the people, slate-gray and sullen. Later it awakes, flashing sunshine, laughing like a strong man delirious with his own strength.

In the heat of the midday the houses appear faded and dry as though they were about to become powder under the calcinating blasts of the sun. By late afternoon the blends of earth colors in the walls are rich and deep, and traces of green can be seen in the straw-tans of the roof thatch. Later, the cooking fires send up plumes of slate-blue smoke, bannering the sky. The people moving about the fires are lustrous black and all the village has the soft delicate texturing of evening.

After having seen and felt and smelled the setting, the forest and the river and the old houses of the village in their many, ever changing aspects, I was ready to watch the exciting event of Quay-Quay's new house mushrooming its fresh erect stalk and cap into the sky. He had bought a cow for the big festivity and Sahda was busy supervising preparations for the feast.

A stake was driven into the earth at the point which
would be the center of their house. A string of twisted
raffia was tied to the stake. At the other end of the string
was a pointed stick. Quay-Quay walked in a circle, keeping the string taut, and scratched the circle where the
walls would rise. All of the people watched this silently.
It had the dignity and formality of the laying of a cor-
nerstone.

Then with a yell of "Ai-i-i-i!" the men dispersed in groups, some to bring in the rattan which had already been cut in the jungle, some to cut the thick logs for the doorways, some to cut the more slender upright sticks, some to bring the long, thin roof poles, others to get the thatch. The small boys brought the twigs, which were to be laced onto the upright poles in a wattle to hold the mud plaster. Women and children carried baskets on their heads to get the clay for plastering from a great termite mound on the edge of the village.

The upright poles were driven into the ground along the scratched surface until the circle was a stockade. The space for the piazza was marked off inside the circle; it did not protrude beyond. The little twigs were laid horizontal and bent to the circle of uprights, being tied securely with rattan at every intersection. Ceiling poles were laid across the top of the structure at wide intervals, and then a thick bundle of twigs, called a "collar," was tied around the top. On this the roof would rest. The long roof poles lay like the ribs of a half-opened umbrella from the tall mastlike center pole of the house. Twigs were bent and tied in ever larger circles onto the roof poles. The men stood on the scaffolding of poles, winding their toes around them, and bending low, quickly tied the knots and yanked them secure. The lighter insides of their palms flashed against the black of their naked bodies as they made motions too quick to follow with the eye. It was like music full of grace notes.

The bundles of glistening still-green thatch were tied into the intersections of twigs with poles deeply overlapping each layer. The completed roof was several inches thick and impervious to the pounding of the sun's rays and rain.

The stems of the top thatch were caught up in a wrapped bundle at the very peak of the house, cresting it with a cylindrical topknot.

While the thatching was progressing, the boys were trampling termite clay for "plaster" with their bare feet. The wet-down mud splashed with the plosh of their broad feet and squirted between the spread toes. They shoved each other and fell down and got up again to playfully shove another into it. They became so covered with the mud that they seemed made of it except for a sudden flash of white teeth and rolling eyes.

The clay was firmly wedged between each stick until it was a solid wall. A good house is rubbed many times. For the final coat a special clay is used which is found by digging deep pits in the earth. Sometimes it is pink, sometimes a golden ocher, sometimes a gray-white. Much care is used in rubbing this final layer and the hands are moved in patterns that are rounded sweeps, while drums beat the rhythm.

The door was cut in one piece from the breastbonelike edge of a tree buttress. After several of these fiber-matted oblongs of wood are taken from a big buttress, the tree has a jack-o-lantern look of missing teeth.

Quay-Quay would paint a colored clay mural on the outside after the house was completely dry. The mural is the exuberance of a house. All else is done in the traditional manner, in the pattern of generations of doing, so that it has come to be considered the only proper way. The mural is a glad burst of individual freedom. He

will think about it a long time before he paints it. He
will certainly include a Ford pickup with rice sacks in
the back, straddled by several native car boys, wearing
skivvy shirts and white duck trousers. The driver will be
a subtly caricatured white man, facing straight ahead in
the tight posture of speed but the eye will be drawn
fullface in the manner of the Egyptians.

Quay-Quay planned another bit of individuality for his
house, a latrine like those he had seen in the plantation
labor camps. It would look like a miniature hut, a baby
toadstool, back of the new house. It would have no raised
bench, only a flat slab with a key-hole shaped opening
above a deep pit. This would have to wait until he had
discussed it with the old men of the tribe. It is the native
custom to go into the bush outside the town to ease the
body and perhaps this "modern" idea would be considered a contamination to the village. New ways had to
be talked of softly-softly.

When the construction was finished Sahda hung her
wind chimes under the eaves, and Quay-Quay's old pa
hung some luck medicine over the door. While the people feasted and danced noisily, I stood in the moonlight
with Sahda to admire her new home.

Part of its beauty was the frank use of the materials.
There was no attempt anywhere to conceal the structure.
One could look up into the steep peak of the roof and
see the flexuous circling of twigs bound against the rib
poles by steely ribbons of rattan. If Sahda ties a mat to
the ceiling poles inside the rooms it will be to form a
storage loft and not to conceal the anatomy of the roof.

The mat will be a beautiful weaving of bamboo, coarse

enough to belong with the mud and thatch. There was no cheating by deception in any part of the house, no pretense. Each part held against every other part because it was tied or smoothed there by human hands. This gave it a fervent quality. Because it was small and the roof had the exceedingly steep pitch of forest houses illustrated in fairy stories, there was a gay (but not giddy) doll-house enchantment about it, a child-quality.

Sahda and I looked and saw that it was good.

"*Inyoms*," she said, and felt for my hand. It is the Vai word for "sister." I was deeply grateful that she did not add *gbema*, which means "white." The happenstance that she had been born with more pigment in her skin than I had nothing to do with it. We were just two women standing there in the moonlight with clasped hands looking at a beautiful new house which would soon be a home.

CHAPTER FIFTEEN

And So What?

IT WAS MORNING of the long-dreamed-about day when
I was going to start through the hinterland to Ganta! In
the filmy cloud of mosquito net above my head, drops of
moisture, which had collected during the night, shone
like crystal. Outside the window, the pepper bird which
awakens West Africa each morning was singing lustily.
The servants began to stir. They knew this was a special
day and they must be up earlier than usual. Johnny and
Buno were going with me. The Kpuesi boys had been
telling Johnny for a week that when he passed through
the Kpuesi nation their devil would drag him off to the
bush, so he had better tell all his Bassau brothers a long
good-bye. If the Kpuesi devil didn't catch him the Mano
devil would, and if the Mano devil didn't get him, he
would fall in the river and the Neji water people would
take him to their underwater village. In any case, he
would never return to the plantation.

Johnny was willing to face these perils for the sake of
the great prestige he would enjoy if he did get back. He
made great drama out of packing his things for the trip.
All his possessions rolled together made one small bundle

which had to be rerolled many times. My own supplies had been packed by our friends the day before amid the flurry of a typical plantation Sunday. Kerosene crates had been filled and battened, lids carpentered, hinges made out of folded country cloth, boxes closed and opened again for additions.

I had been grateful for friends who took the responsibility of seeing that I carried the necessary *things* for the journey. To them the trip was largely a matter of a caravan of essential articles moving over rough trails ahead of me. To me it was something quite different, and I had slight care for what I should take, and little mind to give to it. It was good, then, to have friends who "had sense for travel."

While I had talked to dinner guests who had not left and supper guests who were arriving, and week-end guests whose afternoon siesta had been interrupted, scraps of conversation floated up through the floor from the packers below:

"Now if I were going, I would take —— "

"No, she won't need that, but —— "

"Now listen, you have to travel light on the trail. You can't carry all the comforts of home."

"But even soldiers in battle! Why, it's the most common article found in their pockets."

"Well, they don't carry a whole *roll* of it!"

"Suppose she'd get fever —— "

"A twenty-two's no gun for the trail. We ought to have borrowed a heavy gun."

"Oh, a twenty-two's all right for shooting monkeys for the carriers to eat."

"Well, she's got her forty-five. I told her to carry that on her hip all the time."

"I told her never to try a shot she wasn't sure of in front of a native."

"They say there's plenty bush hog up there."

"They're dangerous. I wish she weren't going to do any hunting."

"I wish she weren't going."

"Oh, she'll be all right. I bet one trip will be enough, though."

"Say, where is her money? She can't use silver up there. She's got to have coppers."

"I wish she would send a runner back every night. Why, if anything would happen, we wouldn't know it for days."

"Sure we would! It would be on the drums in an hour."

"Suppose all the carriers should set down their loads the second day out and melt into the jungle. What would she do then?"

"She ought to have a Liberian soldier to take care of things like that."

"No, she doesn't want the government in on this. And she hasn't got a pass for the interior."

"There ought to be some way to lock the water canteens. The boys are apt to dump the water and carry them empty, and then refill them from a stream."

"No padlocks! I offered two shillings each in my camp yesterday, and didn't get a one."

"Say, where's her drawing stuff? That's the main thing she wants."

"I'll bet it's packed. That's the one thing she would think of."

"There isn't any atabrin in the medicine kit. My God, if we'd forgotten that. . . ."

Finally the pounding had ceased and I was called under the house to inspect twelve cases, complete with labeled initials which had been branded on the sides with hot wires. The "S" in the center was backwards. In addition to twelve Mano carriers, I would have some extra boys to carry the examples of native crafts I hoped to collect en route.

I had slept in spite of the excitement. I pulled back the damp mosquito net and shivered with cold and anticipation as I stepped into the new day.

There was a clatter of boxes being loaded into the pickup under the house. The needless banging and harangue which accompanies this process often annoyed me, but this morning I liked it. I, too, wanted to heave something large and heavy and to make a lot of noise.

"It be my part to carry the Missy's black box," I heard Johnny assert. "Everywhere the Missy go, the black box go also. It stay for my hand. It can't go for the back of the pickup."

"What thing stay inside the black box that Yardboy can't carry?" Buno asked, in a deflated tone.

"Plenty thing stay inside the box," said Johnny in a mysterious and confidential voice. "Medicine for the face live inside! So-so red stick for the mouth, so-so face powder, so-so face grease, and fine scent from the French side. White woman can no be strong for nothing without medicine for the face."

How could Johnny know the courage that comes from a lipstick?

The end of the motor road came sooner than we expected. A bridge had been out north of Kakata for some time, and we had been crossing on a temporary structure. Now the new bridge was finished and the temporary one had been removed.

A wild-eyed Liberian soldier waved his arms frantically to bar our way.

"Wait, Boss! Wait!" he cried. "You can't pass this side."

"How we can't pass for the other side? The new bridge fini, no' so?"

"Oh, huh, the new bridge, he fini, for true, but the President no bless the bridge until tomorrow-time."

"But we can't wait for tomorrow-time. The way we go be far, to Ganta self. How we can manage?"

"Well, Ma, the thing you can do, yah, you sit down here small. One truck stay for the other side to carry people to Salala. Soon-time, he can come here to carry you."

The only thing to do was to unload all our cargo and sit down to wait for the truck. One hour, two hours went by. The sun was hot. I found shelter in an old carpenter shed and stretched out on the carpenter's bench to rest. I dozed and was awakened by what I thought was rain falling on my face and legs. I was stiff and sore from sleeping on the hard bench. When I sat up to stretch the kinks out of my spine, I saw that the gentle rain was a shower of small brown pellets falling out of the thatch roof above my head.

Cockroaches! Millions of cockroaches eating the thatch in the roof! I sat up wide-eyed, and the pellets rattled from me like shot.

A few hours ago, I thought, I awoke to the splendor of crystal gems of dew caught in the white cloud of mosquito net. Now I awake to reality. Reality is the excrement of cockroaches falling on my face. The trip was getting off to a bad start.

As the hot, tedious hours passed, crowds collected under the shade of the carpenter's roof. A gaunt Mandingo in flowing white robe and baggy trousers sat apart from the others on a pile of lumber and stared straight ahead into the shimmering heat. Men sighed as they reached the shade, and took huge loads from their heads or long *kinjas* from their backs. I watched the growing number of people with apprehension. There seemed to be several truckloads instead of just one.

The sun was slanting obliquely on the flat-topped bedi trees when I finally heard the snorting of an overloaded motor. The miserable truck arrived with a burst of speed and skidded to a stop in a cloud of dust. It looked something like a decrepit school bus with a canvas top and no doors in the rear. Out of the swirling dust, people and animals emerged with the violence of an explosion. Naked small boys shot out through the window holes. Chickens, flying feathers, bleating goats, one squealing pig, chattering women with pickins pancaked against their backs, old men with canes, Mandingos with ballooning trousers, and porters with loads still on their heads popcorned out of the dim interior.

The people who had been waiting all day to get aboard

the truck surged forward and collided with those who were getting off, bumping their bodies and their loads. Standing on the edge of this swirl of humanity was like being on the fringe of a tornado.

Maybe I could charter the truck for a special trip.

The driver sat under the steering wheel as though all that was happening was beneath his concern. He was a pompous Americo-Liberian, and wore an old black coat and a newly whitened sun helmet which he lifted with exaggerated courtesy as I approached.

"What may I do for you, Madame?" he asked in over-articulated English.

"I would like to charter the truck to make a trip to Salala to carry me and my carriers and loads," I explained.

"You will have to care for your business with the purser," he said, replacing his helmet as though the interview were finished. "It is barely possible the matter could be arranged for a suitable honorarium."

"Where can we find the purser?" I asked.

"Really, Madame, the whereabouts of my colleague is of no concern to me. Perhaps you may discover him in the regions behind the truck."

The purser was finally discovered a quarter of a mile down the road, drinking cane-juice rum on the piazza of a mud hut.

"Good afternoon," he said thickly.

"I would like to charter the truck," I said.

"I do not own yonder vehicle. Such matters are under the jurisdiction of the owner."

"Where is the owner?"

"He is residing at present, I believe, in the hinterland city of Salala, which, I presume, is your destination."

"I have made strong medicine for this journey," I said, in a voice that I hoped would carry through the fog of his drunkenness. "I carry my medicine on my hip. You will go with me to the driver, and we will talk the charter palaver with him."

He looked blearily at the forty-five and rubbed his mouth with his sleeve. To my surprise, he put the bottle of cane juice in his pocket and without another word walked ahead of me toward the truck. The incident did not seem melodramatic at the time. It was only afterwards that I felt like a female Jesse James.

"I have arranged with the purser to charter the truck," I said to the driver. "I will pay him one pound, five. You can carry as many of the other people as can get aboard. Perhaps all can ride if the loads are stacked tightly instead of thrown in helter-skelter."

The driver shrugged the matter from his dusty shoulders. He made no reply.

"Buno!" I shouted.

Buno came out of the back of the truck where he had wormed his way.

"Yeah, Ma?"

"Tell all the people in Kpuesi that they must come down, together with all their loads, from inside the truck."

People and loads and animals obediently tumbled out. My carriers stacked their cases compactly against the rear of the cab, and stood tightly against them.

"All right, Buno! Tell the people that all who can get inside can go to Salala in the truck we charter."

I watched unbelievingly as every person, goat, and chicken in the road was swallowed up in the maw of the truck.

As I climbed into the cab beside the driver, I was glad that everyone could go to Salala in one trip. No doubt the journey of each person seemed as important and urgent to him as mine did to me. If I had waited for a second trip, the truck would never have come back to me, and if any of the natives had had to wait, there would have been palaver about who was entitled to preference.

The seat in the cab was a long board. I sat between the driver and the drunken purser. A Liberian, who of course would not lower himself to ride with the natives, sat on the outside. He had a bottle labeled in ink, "Nerve medicine," from which he took constant swigs. After each fortification from the bottle, he repeated wearily, "And so what?" The cab had no doors, and if any of the four persons on the board seat fell out, it would be the driver or Mr. And-So-What.

We were off to Salala with a deafening salute from the exploding exhaust. We careened around corners so fast that I thought everyone in the cab would be slung out in the bushes. We chugged through mud holes, but the tops of the hills were dusty. We speeded up for the plank bridges. Perhaps the driver thought he was more likely to hit the three or four planks and stay on them if he got it over with in a hurry. When we lurched into washed-out gullies running diagonally across the road, I expected the creaking truck to split apart like a ripe melon, tossing people into the air lightly as black seeds.

The truck groaned. Its anguished frame must never have known a grease gun. At every crisis, Mr. And-So-What took a swig from his bottle. He had difficulty connecting with his mouth between jolts. I had noticed while the truck was being loaded that "And-So-What?" was the name of the vehicle, lettered on the side with red lead in a mixture of capitals and lower-case letters. The phrase repeated over and over by the Liberian, the set and shrug of the driver's shoulders, the defiance with which he attacked all the hazards of the road with a burst of speed, seemed to leave everything to Fate. I found it impossible to do this as I braced the palms of my hands against the rusty dashboard to keep from being hurtled against the windshield. I remembered that part of the news I heard almost every week from my servants was an account of another wreck of a shilling truck.

We roared into Salala with a burst of speed and much bleating of the shrill klaxon on the truck, scattering dogs and sheep and goats and children from the dusty street where they had been dozing in the sun.

Several of my carriers who had started ahead of me and were to meet me in Salala waited with Saga, the headman.

"Let's go, Saga," I said. "My heart is hungry for the trail."

"Ma," Saga mourned, "some palaver catch we for this town. The chief of Salala set tomorrow time to hear the palaver. Sometime, it can take all day; sometime, it can take the week to throw cold water on an old palaver."

"What bad thing the men do to bring palaver on their heads in this town?" I asked. I had visions of sitting down a week in the filthy noisy village.

"Ma, this be a thing that cannot fall for your ear," Saga said sadly.

"Saga," I said firmly, "I agree for you to sleep here, one night only. Myself, I will take Buno and Johnny and Comma and go to Poland plantation to sleep. But soon-morning time and you no come, oh, how I can vex! You tell the chief he must talk the palaver this night-time. He no fini, ah hah! that long white ma that buy chicken-egg here every week and do plenty good thing for the chief, she can throw vex for the chief self. You hear me good, man?"

"I hear you good, Ma Warner. So I tell the chief."

Saga marshaled his nondescript crew who started off to the chief's house, single file.

I sorted out the cases we would need for cooking and for sleeping and started to the Polish plantation, two hours down the trail. Buno objected to leaving at the late hour.

"We beg you, let us stay," he said. "Some hellova big palaver can be talked here. We want to hear."

The path to the Polish plantation was smooth except for the swamps. We crossed these on laced twigs, which let the muck come through ankle-deep but kept us from sinking deeper. It was almost dark when we turned from the trail and entered the plantation of coffee trees and palms. The young Poles who had started the project had been recalled to Poland to help fight the war. Vines had overrun the trees and bound them to the earth. Nature

had blanketed down the entire plantation against the return of the young men who had started this garden in the
jungle.

The large mud house with a corrugated-iron roof was
unlocked. We pushed open the heavy black-gum doors,
and the musty closed-up air hit us like a weight. We

flashed the interior with our torches, and several disturbed bats were caught in the beams of light. Cobwebs hung like curtains from the mat ceilings, and rats scurried above the matting.

We lighted two lanterns and found enough wood to make a good fire in the center of the concrete floor. Buno swept down cobwebs with a broom of switches. As the smoke of the fire filtered through the mat ceiling, small animals scurried out under the eaves.

There were three rooms. The boys built their own fire on the floor and soon had cassava roasting in the embers.

"Put cassava in your fire for my part also," I told them. I had not eaten since breakfast.

Johnny and Buno hung my hammock and mosquito net from the ceiling and Comma brought water from the creek to boil for the next day's drinking supply.

A day had passed. I had made only about eight miles on the long trek across the country. How many days would be required to resolve Saga's palaver in Salala?

I thought we might as well clean the place up in the morning and prepare to sit down a week or so. Sometimes a chief won't hear a palaver until all the people who want to attend have had time to assemble.

If only I could apply the philosophy of Mr. And-So-What to our journey! My feet itched for the trail. Well, the hunting was said to be good on the Gbong mountains against which the plantation nestled, and in the morning I would see what meat I could shoot. If I were lucky, I would send a dash to the chief of Salala to open his ears to quick talk.

CHAPTER SIXTEEN

What Ye Have Gained in a Day

THE TAT-A-TAT of rain on the corrugated-iron roof of the plantation house awakened me to a wet dawn. Last night's fire was a heap of dead ashes and the gray ends of the unburned sticks. The hammock ropes had stretched, allowing the net to sag. My blankets were in a wad around my middle. The smell of mold was heavy suffocation in every breath of air. I pulled my feet under the damp blankets and shivered.

Comma rushed in out of the rain and shook my hammock to waken me. For Comma to rush anywhere was unusual. As his name implied, he was in a continuous state of pause. Some of the boys pronounced it "Coma," which was even more appropriate. Rain ran out of his hair into rivulets down his back and chest. His skin which usually glistened a rich red umber was cold gray, and goose pimples stood high on his chest.

"Missy! I find meat! Come shoot for we. I beg you, Missy. Fine small deer sleep for one cassava farm. I go look for chicken-egg for Missy breakfast, and I put my eye on the deer through the leaves."

Cold and damp as my blankets were, they seemed more desirable than the rain outside. Comma's eyes were pleading.

"I beg you, Missy!"

"All right, I come. Go wake Buno. Tell him make the fire live. So soon we come back it is necessary to dry my clothes."

"I go wake Johnny, Missy. Let Buno go with we. Buno can be strong to carry back the meat."

It did not seem to occur to Comma that I might not bring down meat. He led Buno and me confidently to the cassava patch a couple of miles away. The chill rain pounded us so violently I thought my bombarded skin would respond with dull thuds, but I heard only the sopping of my feet in wet sandals and the swish of dripping bushes against my gabardine trousers.

"There, Missy! There! Shoot!" Comma pointed and whispered. I could see nothing through the curtain of rain except the dim outline of wet cassava plants.

"I can't see anything, Comma."

"Something steal your eye, Missy. I see the deer good. Set your eye hard, Missy." Comma pointed desperately.

"Look! He turns his head now," Buno whispered in my other ear. "God tells him, 'Take care, yah.'"

I forced my vision with all my will but I could see nothing at which to aim. There was a rustle and cracking of cassava stems as something bounded away.

"Gone," Buno said sorrowfully. "Come see the place where the deer take cassava-leaf chop and lie him down to sleep."

Comma and Buno exchanged puzzled glances and led

me to the nestlike resting place where the deer had spent the night.

"Missy?"

"Yes, Comma?"

"Could it be that Missy look on the lightning in the night?"

"No, Comma, I sleep the whole night."

"Yesterday-time, could Missy put her eye to the sun's face?"

"No, Comma, it is only that God give black man to see in the bush past white man," I said.

"I think, Missy," said Comma, "that God give black man, and white man, all, two good eye to see in the bush, but white man let his good eye waste."

The unhappiness I felt as I sloshed back to camp was not all from being miserably cold and wet. How I envied these black people their vision! First, I had coveted their discriminating way of looking at things which enabled them to carve and design with elemental force. Now I had learned that I could not distinguish even the outlines of an animal which was perfectly clear to Buno and Comma. I had good eyes but I didn't know how to use them. How much I must be missing when I walked down the forest paths! Oh, that the world in which I walked could be truly revealed to me through my eyes and ears and nostrils and fingertips! Or that I had not discovered how little I saw of what might be seen. I remembered some verses from the Koran:

> Say, "Look you now, if God should catch your hearing and your sight, and should set a seal upon your hearts — who is good but God to bring you it again?" [and]

With Him are the keys of the unseen. He it is who takes
you to Himself at night, and knows what ye have gained in
the day; then He raises you up again, that your appointed
time may be fulfilled; then unto Him is your return, and
then will He inform you of what ye have done.

The rain slackened a little before we reached the
house. Johnny had a roaring fire on the piazza and a
smaller one in the room where I had slept. I changed
into dry clothes and sat over the fire, drinking many cups
of tea.

"Where did you get dry wood?" I asked.

"Missy," Johnny said, "the Poland men leave before
their good wood finish. Even white-man war cannot wait
for people to sit long by the fire. So it is with our people,
also."

I went into the room where the boys had slept. On
top of the flat desk were photographs of families, and one
of a young man with his arm around a girl. A package
of hastily opened letters in Polish lay under a sifting of
dust and spiderwebs.

I dusted the desk and the photographs. It was a futile
act, but at the moment it seemed the only thing I could
do for the girl in the snapshot.

The sun came out hotly on the wet leaves. The mists
cleared from the Gbong mountains in great swirls of
white veil-like clouds. All the earth steamed and grew.
The rustle of small animals under the cover crop seemed
almost the sound of vines growing and binding more
tightly the overrun palms and coffee trees to the solid
earth.

Saga arrived with his men just before noon. Each was heavily loaded with the cargo he was to carry upcountry. Pads of vines cushioned the friction against their skulls. Two men carried drums of benzene on their heads. All the loads weighed at least sixty pounds, but some were more unwieldy than others.

"Palaver fini!" Saga announced triumphantly.

"Any man held for hostage?" I asked.

"No, Ma, all we here."

"Let's go, then."

"Ma," Saga said, "we never take chop since yesterday-time. You see the big hill there? Empty stomach make weak back. Rice puts iron in the legs. The men can no carry over the hill of Chief Repu without they eat."

When the men had eaten and gone ahead of me down the path, I closed the heavy door of the plantation house. The young Poles who closed it for the last time before going away must have turned and looked at it as I was doing, wanting to remember the beautiful red brown of the gumwood set into the yellow ocher of the clay walls. Down the path a way, I turned and looked back at the yellow house against the vibrant green jungle-covered mountain. The mountain seemed close and clear-cut in the flood of yellow sunlight. The mists were just above the highest trees. With my back to the matted plantation, I could be glad for the perfect composition and color of the whole scene. Acting on a sudden impulse, I ran back to the house and wrote a bad couplet on the yellow wall of the piazza with my lipstick:

> The sun is shining on the mountains of Gbong;
> My heart with the mist is rising in song.

The rains and the sun will eventually erase the lipstick, which is well. It was a poor barter that I left behind — only some bad verse and a woman's touch on a dusty desk. I carried with me a singing hope that the prayer which had cried from my heart in the morning rain to Allah, whom I call God, would be each day answered in small part and that when he took me to himself at night he and I would know that I had gained a little in that day!

The sun was scorching. We steamed with the vegetation as we began the climb up Repu. Then rain fell again. Water poured down over the rocks of Repu so fast that climbing them was like climbing a waterfall. Streams of water poured off the tops of the rocks on our heads, hit at our necks as we raised ourselves by grasping small tree trunks, shot at our stomachs. Feet slipped. Hands slipped. Water struggle! Rock struggle! Jagged rocks. Feet cut, hands cut, back wrenched! Blood, red on hands and feet and washed out to pink by streams of water! The awful feeling of a nightmare when one runs and runs and gets nowhere.

The moment I stopped to gasp for air, bracing my back on the uphill side of a tree so I could not slip back, I froze with cold. I looked for the carriers but I could not see them. The last time I had looked around Johnny was only a few feet behind me, the outline of his body a gray blur through the rain.

On, then. Almost the top? No, there was more. But not so much hauling of oneself up rocks. Better toeholds. The slope became a little less steep. A flat rock under a great Cola tree! The grave of Chief Repu, who was mighty to his people as the great mountain.

I flung myself down flat on my face on the rock, too exhausted to take another step. My heart felt bursting. Breathing was a horrible pain that had to go on. Like a drowning person who wants to sleep under the water, I wanted to stay on the rock and let the rain beat my body to numbness to stop the pain of breathing. I, who had prayed to become sentient, now wanted to renounce feeling, to become as unfeeling as the flat rock where I lay. My hands dangled inert in the mud on either side of the stone. My fingertips, through which so much that was meaningful had come to me, were the last of my body to let go of awareness. Finally they, too, were free of feeling and lay in the mossy slime. A darkness closed mercifully over me, as black as that which covered old Repu asleep under the rock.

A mighty cola tree had grown from the seed planted in Repu's grave; the slime was fertile. Birds in the top branches of the cola could see over the next hill. The warm darkness became gray, wet light and my hands and legs became my own again. Ahead was the top of the mountain. The coastal plain was behind and beneath me. The stone on Repu's grave was the threshold over which I had stepped into the interior of Africa!

The blur beside me was Johnny. He shouted above the roar of the rain, "Don't stop, Missy. One hut live over the top of the mountain. We can go there, make fire and get dry."

The woman in the hut opened her door to us and we spread our hands above the fire in the center of the floor. My tin trunk had shed water but a heavy stench of mold fumed at me as I shook out clean clothes. Dry woolen clothing against a rain-shriveled skin! Healing ointment and clean bandages on stinging cuts. Fire warmth and wool warmth and welcome warmth in the smiling eyes of the black woman!

I wanted to fall into a hammock, but my muscles were tense and cramped. I eased myself gradually to a horizontal position, wondering if we would have to sit down all the next day to thaw the stiffness beside a fire.

"Ma?" Saga was knocking at the door.

"Yes, Saga?"

"Ma, all we need medicine for the feet. Plenty bad thing catch we today. We beg you for the grease for the feet."

I squeezed ointment out of a tube onto a paper and handed it to Saga.

"Missy, take your shoes inside the net," Johnny said. "Outside, scorpions can live there before morning."

Drowsiness flowed with healing over my aches, releasing my mind from the necessity of thinking about them, allowing me to float in space over the distance ahead.

Tomorrow, when I traveled over those hills with difficulty instead of in floating drowsiness, I would not be disappointed; today had proven that each day fulfills itself.

Rocks and mountains and oozing swamp mud were no longer inert to me after they had caught and slowed and inflicted pain on my body.

"When we shook the mountains over them as though it were a shadow," the Prophet had said. The words were alive now because I had been hurt by the shaking mountain. Truly, when God takes you to himself at night, he lets you know what you have gained in a day!

"Saga," I asked the next morning, "the men fit to walk the trail?"

"Yeah, Ma," Saga replied. "The trail that beat the foot is medicine for the foot also. The man that can let the town hold him for sore foot can't go nowhere. Let go, yah?"

I hoped that there was medicine in the trail for my own bruised feet, as I stumbled around preparing for the day.

Before we had gone far, the chant of the carriers changed from a walking song into a loud "Yaw! Yaw! Yah!" There were overtones of fear and dread and a bit of bravado in it.

"There is something ahead on the trail to match strength against," I thought.

"Yaw! Yaw!" There was a new sound in the chant now, a faint sound of faraway rushing water. It blended and became one with the carriers' song, until the voices and the rushing water trembled in unison like an organ peal.

When I stood on the bank of the stream with the carriers I saw the swift greenish current swirling and roaring, carrying logs and small trees with it. An empty canoe whirled past. Had it cut loose from its bank tie, or had the Neji, the water people, been hungry?

"How can we manage, Saga?" I asked. "No good place here to make camp."

"We can cross, Ma," Saga said confidently. He spoke in Mano to the men, who took off the few clothes they had been wearing and made them into a single bundle which one of them tied to his neck.

Only the small country-cloth pouches containing their luck medicine and their small carved personal masks remained on the glistening bodies. They tied the leather cords that held these tightly around their necks, after each had reached his fingers into the bag to rub the forehead of his mask in prayer. I found myself wishing there

were a symbol in my hands, something shiny and hard
to grasp. Though prayer is good, a spirit cannot be held
in empty trembling fingers.

The hammock frame which had been brought for emer-
gencies was carried to the bank. It resembled the roof of
a doghouse, two steep planes meeting in a ridge in the
center and covered over with bamboo matting. One man
stood under each corner, resting the weight on his head.

"Go for the top-side, Ma," Saga commanded.

I climbed on a stump to mount the roof. I was so stiff
that Saga had to push me from the stump. I straddled
the sharp center ridge with difficulty. The mat was slippery and there was no hand hold to grasp. I pressed my
knees against the mat and tried to brace my feet on a
board along the bottom of the gable.

My "horses" started down the steep slippery bank
holding the frame on their heads with braced arms. The
two front men were up to their hips in water before the
rear two left the bank. The pitch of the roof was steep.
The back part of me would not stay *back!* Knees and
hands slipped forward and I was sure I would be pitched
over the end into the swirling water. How lightly I
would be tossed up and borne under and tossed again by
the swirling water. I could not swim in such swift current. A dead goat and another log floated by. Perhaps
the men would think that the Neji wanted me, should I
fall over the end of the frame. Would they make any
effort to rescue me? I was small and weak against the
bigness of the water.

When it seemed I could not hold the perch another
second, the frame leveled out a little and I could push

back my sliding weight. One man walked ahead of the four. He probed for holes with a long pole. The men went deeper and deeper into the water. It was up to their chins and around their mouths. One who was shorter than the others went in over his head and I could see only his swelling arm muscles still clinging to his corner of the frame as he swam. A great log churned downstream behind us, almost knocking against the bodies of the two men in the rear.

When we were finally across, I slid off the frame into the arms of the man who had walked ahead with the pole. He grinned at me, happily.

"God bless we, Ma."

Johnny, who would not take off his trousers, had lost them in midstream. The bundle of extra clothes tied to his neck was soaked.

The Manos considered this a fine joke on the uppity Bassau boy. Johnny kept what dignity he could and made modest use of his long wet shirttail as we stood around a fire to dry.

"Missy," he said. "Our people have a country saying."

"What is the saying, Johnny?"

"Rain-time River say, 'I never put eye on a tall man!' Missy self, is not tall to that river. For myself, no boy feels tall without trouser."

We walked in sticky swamps knee-deep in mud. I crossed narrow streams "pick-a-back" on men's shoulders. At one narrow, deep gorge where the water came up to the men's chins, I got on top of a tall man's shoulders and hung on by clutching him under the chin with my hands and locking my heels across his chest. The other men stood shoulder to shoulder across the stream in water up to their necks, and pulled me from one man to the next so that I would not be swept downstream. When I was across, my carrier bent over and I slipped to a log over his head.

Darkness caught us at Bondoi, a couple of hours from Suokoko, where I wanted to spend the night at a mission. How good it would be to sleep in a bed and sit at a table with a white tablecloth! Carriers bringing Mano rice downcountry were sleeping at Bondoi, and my Mano men wanted to spend the night there with their good friends and country brothers. They exchanged greetings as though they had not seen each other for years, instead of a few days. Palaver was gathering.

The only way I will get to Suokoko tonight is to throw a vex, I thought.

The vex must have been convincing. We staggered on to Suokoko. The last mile seemed more than I could manage.

"Just one more step," I would tell myself. "Think only of the next step. I can always take *one* more. Don't think it is eight miles; think only of one more step."

When we reached Suokoko, I learned that the Mission was beyond the town about a mile.

My legs seemed to swing from my hips on rusty wires in the manner of an old doll's. I sat down for a minute on a log, knowing that it was a mistake. The only way was to keep going.

Johnny came limping over to me and took my hand in his.

"Hold tight to my hand, my Missio," he said. "Small strength can go from me to you through my hand."

It was all I could do to get up from the log even with Johnny to pull against.

"You limp badly, Johnny."

"Yeah, Missy. When a Bassau boy puts on shoes, it is to be a big man, and walking the trail is not for a big man."

"Wear your shoes on your head. Then all the people can see that you have shoes but they will not catch your feet."

"Missy, when any man becomes a big man, there will be some hurt come with it. It is better that my feet hurt than I catch hurt from the laugh of the people who wear no shoes. Enough that the bad river steal my best trouser. What you call this thing in English, Missy?"

"The English word is 'pride,' Johnny. It often has to do with aching feet. It catch plenty Missy in my own country."

"Then, Missy, I think I will learn to let hurt catch my feet. It must be that this is a civilized thing."

We were a bedraggled lot that knocked on the door of the Mission house at nine o'clock. The Nickersons greeted us warmly. The carriers were given rice and sent to a shelter. In the living room, I met Lucille Price, a nurse from my home town in Iowa.

We snapped fingers in the native fashion.

"*Aye-O-Gbagviah!*" she returned my Gio greeting. I gave her year-old messages from her family who lived near mine.

"Tell me the news of our home town," she said.

Iowa seemed a distant place I remembered rather vaguely, and I could think of nothing at all to say about Marshalltown. The gray stone courthouse that had seemed so magnificent to me when I was a child had been dwarfed by the mountains of Gbong. The Victorian grandeur of the big houses along West Main Street had been curtained off by a screen of rain and the smoke of little fires in mud huts where I had found shelter. It was

more natural to say "Gbagviah" than to give any other
greeting, more instinctive now to snap fingers than to
shake hands. "Gbagviah" to the Gios, "Moin" to the
Bassaus, "Ca-u-ah" to the Manos, "Yah-nah" to the
Buzis, "Salaam Alaikim" to the Mohammedans! Those
were the ways of greeting. How hollow it would sound
were I to hear "How do you do?" after having heard the
"Peace be with you" and having seen the touching of
hearts of the Mandingos meeting on the trail. The chair
where I sat was for me, and for each of us who sat in the
room, on the right side of the curtain of rain and smoke.

CHAPTER SEVENTEEN

Chicken Blood and Chamber Music

Ma, the men beg you to sit down one day," old Saga pleaded the next morning. "Our strength fini."

My strength was finished too. I was glad to sit down.

The Manos went into the village of Suokoko to look up old friends, but Johnny would not leave the mission.

Saga came back with exciting news.

"The blacksmith die-o!" he announced.

"What thing catch him?" asked Mr. Nickerson.

"The blacksmith break taboo," Saga said. "The blacksmith he big man for Devil bush, but not even blacksmith self can play with the Bush Society. Last night time when the blacksmith sleep, one country hand axe jump from the man's tools on the fanner where they stay on the floor of the work kitchen. It catch the man on the head and knock him ti' he dead. Myself, I see just now how the hand axe fit the place the man be knock. After he fini, the hand axe, he go back to the fanner, but he can't lie him down in straight line with other tool; he stay for top-side. The blacksmith's tool, he great past blacksmith self."

"All the people believe the tool knock him?" I asked Saga.

"Well, Ma, so the people say," Saga replied. Then, whispering, "Sometime, the old man in the Devil Society can speak small to the tool."

Saga looked over his shoulder to see if he were quite alone with us. An old Mano carrier stood behind him, scowling fiercely. Saga turned on his heel and walked away.

"What do you think really happened?" I asked Mr. Nickerson.

"Probably the big man or elders of the Devil Society decided the blacksmith should be done away with. Many of the blacksmith's tools are considered to have power in their own right. Some of the tools are sacred. It is natural for the common people of the tribe to believe that a tool could jump up by itself and kill the blacksmith. It is because the people believe so strongly in their medicine, that the medicine works."

We went out to the unfinished dispensary which was being built of sun-baked mud bricks. It was being used, although the thatch roof had not been added. People lay on the mats in the sun waiting for their turn to receive the magic needle. Most of them were victims of yaws. The soles of their feet were pitted with deep, festering cavities. One man had lost the entire side of his face, leaving the gums and teeth exposed. In their hands, the patients clasped their paper dispensary tickets. Many of the tickets were bloodstained.

"The people sacrifice chickens and let the blood run

on the tickets," Lucille explained. "They think of the white man's medicine in the same light in which they think of their own medicine, so it is natural that they should pray to the paper and sacrifice to it."

After sleeping two nights in a good bed, I was fit for the trail again. We started early and walked at an even, rapid pace. We passed many broken towns. The roofs had fallen at crazy angles over the crumbled mud walls. Vines matted the whole to the earth. Only the clumps of bananas back of the huts were erect; everywhere else a heavy hand seemed to have flattened everything. Plants grew between the black rocks where food had been cooked. Young trees had cracked through the hard-packed earth in the compound where naked children used to flick their spinning tops with long whips. A rectangle of blackened posts marked the spot of the palaver house where the chief had sat and talked his many palavers. The roof had been burned and the charred posts against the sky were like black snag teeth in the mouth of an old cola-chewing woman.

The arch of stones that must stand until a town falls had been knocked into a heap. Lianas bound the stones together.

The odor of a broken town is different from that of a lively village. Instead of the smells of wood fires burning, and herds of goats, and the living smell of active people, there is the fetid stench of decaying wood and lush fungi and rotting thatch. How long had the people been gone, and why had they left, and where were they now?

"Why the people go from the town?" I asked Saga.

He did not answer, but his face set in a grim mold of hate. He seemed to be thinking as he walked along beside me in silence.

"Listen, Ma!" he said, finally.

We stopped on the trail. There was a sound in the air like the surge of a distant river. The sound was an angry sort of restlessness, made audible. Saga pointed at a black blot on the red trail. A narrow ribbon of inky color stretched into the jungle on both sides of the trail.

"Driver ants!" Saga explained. "Now I can show you how it is with we."

Where the ribbon was narrow, a band of soldier ants guarded both edges, and the mass of ants moved between like a sticky, viscous fluid.

"Something catch them here," Saga pointed at the blot where the band had been disrupted. Hundreds of ants milled aimlessly about.

"The government has soldiers, same like the ants. The soldiers come and take our tax money. They come and take our rice and our chickens and our goats. They come to make we carry the government loads and they give we no chop for the trail. They come and tell we to build government roads. They give we nothing but the leather whip on the back for our pay. Our people have to carry chop to we or we die for empty belly. We move like the ants between the soldiers. The people leave the broken towns you see because too many people have to build the road with the red blood on their backs for pay."

"Look, Saga," I said, "there are many ants and few soldiers. So it is with your people also. Not so?"

"So it is," Saga replied. "But all the ants belong to

one tribe. Not so with we. The Manos, the Gios, the Kpuesi, the Buzis, the Kru, the Bassaus, all different, different tribes. All speak different, and one cannot hear another. Every tribe fear the other tribe past the way they can fear the government. One man cannot pass through another nation's country alone. One ant cannot leave the others and go alone in the bush. The government has got guns. No guns stay for our towns. When we want to make war for the government, we move so." He pointed to the ants milling in a circle.

What Saga had said was true. The natives of the hinterland were powerless. All they could do was to disappear into the jungle where the government soldiers could not penetrate, and build new villages hidden from the trails.

Where was the ribbon of ants going and where would they find living food to devour? The individual ant doesn't have to think about it. All he has to do is to follow the ant in front of him, and keep within the boundary of the soldiers' claws.

I slept that night in a village owned by a Liberian. He was as unlike the Liberians I had met previously as are the tribesmen.

Mr. X's village looked like any native village, except that here there was more activity. The wives, who were native women, were filling an empty benzene drum with palm oil. Little girls were bringing vegetables from the fields, and dyeing thread. There were great fanners heaped with indigo dye balls in front of the houses. Spun and dyed thread was stretched on the fences back of the compound. The headwife sat like a queen in the palaver kitchen and directed the hum of activity. She was extremely beautiful, but her beauty was more in her dignity and self-assurance than in her features.

Mr. X came out of the peanut fields to greet us after the headwife had sent a small girl to fetch him. He wore faded blue overalls and a denim shirt and was bare-headed. His handshake was hearty and there was hospitality in his greeting. There was a simple dignity about him that was reminiscent of that of an Iowa farmer.

"I am sorry the big house isn't finished," he said. "We laid out our fields here and planted them before we built our own quarters. The kerosene refrigerator and the good furniture are still at the old farm. But we'll make you as comfortable as we can."

I ate with him on the piazza of the unfinished house. We were served by three of his wives. The table linen was hand-woven country cloth. The china was simple and good.

There was chicken and rice and gravy and green beans, and a new Chinese yam, similar to a white potato. We talked of the agricultural possibilities for Liberia, of his plans for his farm, of the new varieties of disease-resistant foodstuffs he was growing, of places he had been in Europe.

"Why do you farm so far away from the coast?" I asked. "It must be very expensive to send all of your produce down country on men's heads."

"Partly, it's because the soil is good here," he said. "But that's really only an excuse. I like the jungle all about me. My life here is, for me, the way to live."

"A man is fortunate who can live in the way he likes," I said. "It comes to very few."

"I know that," he said, "and I am grateful. I lack none of the comforts here and I am troubled by none of the vexations that usually accompany a comfortable life. I have a refrigerator and am spared a telephone. I have a record player and many good records. I plant much seed and it grows. My wives weave good cloth and cook good food. I have many healthy children. Out there, I have the jungle. What more could any man want?"

We talked away the hours. He spoke English and French fluently, but with none of the flowering phrases and Latin mottoes of which the coast Liberians are so fond. He was the only Liberian I had met who called any wild plant or animal by its correct name. He was also the first one in my experience who believed working in the soil with his own hands had as much dignity as reading law or preaching with Old Testament fury. His education was more complete than my own. He discussed music and played records of some of his favorites from the masters. What impressed me most was his appreciation of the native ways and skills. This appreciation had extended to marrying native women.

The sun was reddening the east when I finally went to my hut. Johnny was sitting on the doorstep wrapped in his bed blanket and deep gloom.

"What trouble catch you, Johnny?" I asked.

"Missy, this is a bad place."

"What's wrong with the place? The people do fine things here."

"Missy, they have got a bad thing here."

"What kind of bad thing?"

"Something they call 'curfew,' Missy. The meaning of

it is this. All we put chop in the fire. All we hungry. The chop lack small to finish cook, and the sun lack small to sleep. Then the watchman come. He take the chop from the fire and kick the fire till the fire die out. He say the big man here can allow no man outside the hut after the sun sleep. The reason is that he do' want no man to humbug his plenty wife. I tell the watchman I be small-boy and my hungry is for rice, but the watchman do' care. He waste the rice. All day we walk in the sun and never eat. A curfew, Missy, is a very bad thing. I think it must be a civilized idea, because the big man here is civilized, but myself, I can't care for that one. My belly talk against that kind of civilize."

"Come inside," I said. "I look for small civilized chop so you can sleep against the talk of your belly. Tomorrow, the men can cook before we start."

When I was finally under my mosquito net, I heard the Victrola playing again, from the piazza of my host's hut, Chamber music dripping pitifully thin into the silence of the African night. I thought of the chicken blood sacrificed on the dispensary tickets. Both had this in common: they were building something fine and new on the foundation of the old. In this way of doing, there might come the answer to the problem of the milling ants which Saga had shown me on the trail.

CHAPTER EIGHTEEN

I Find People

IN THE HEAT of the day, a haze that seems the formidable indifference of Africa screens the horizon. It represents the distances it cloaks. It hangs over the place you are walking toward.

You turn from the veiled distance and watch the carriers ahead of you. You see the forward thrust of bodies under loads, necks bent under the weights on heads, the veins standing out, the bellies drawn tight and panting, legs wide apart, bracing the bodies, the load-sweat flowing from gleaming drops into rivulets, the faces void of expression. You are walking then, not toward a place, but toward night. Night, rice, and a place beside a small fire! Walking, walking toward night, sweet night, when heads can be free of the burdens that crush the aching muscles into bulging swells!

You do not feel tall or smart as you watch the cases that mean your comfort and prestige weighting the carriers ahead of you. The size of your body and spirit has been measured against the infinite haze of distance, measured against the length of the land.

The longest part of a journey is often the last few miles. This was true of the trek to Ganta. A road had been built from the mission to the St. John River, a distance of twenty miles. I had sent the swiftest of my carriers on ahead to Ganta with a drum of benzene in the hope that Doctor Harley could meet me at the river in his pickup. Twenty miles could mean either a big half-day walk on unshaded road, or a half-hour ride in a car.

The St. John River, a boundary of the Mano tribe's territory, is crossed by a long suspension bridge made of knotted lianas. It is anchored on either side of the river to the trunks of great trees by thick cables of twisted vines. A ladder of tied sticks against the tree leads up to the network.

"Spider Devil build the bridge," the carriers told me. "When he work on it, all of the women and children have to stay inside their huts, no person can walk the path."

Saga helped me climb the ladder to the bridge. How had the men who carried Doctor Harley's dismantled pickup across the country managed to get it across the Devil's spiderweb? No wonder they had made the event into a story to tell at their tall-story contests. The teller never won with this tale; it was *true,* fantastic though it was.

The hammocklike structure swayed and bounced beneath my feet as I moved cautiously forward. I thought of the Moslem belief that a man must cross to Paradise on a narrow cord guided by a beam of light from a friendly angel, a cord on which the good will find steady footing,

but from which the evil will slip and hurtle into a seething hell below. When the Mandingos tell the tale, it is
the greedy Neji of the pagan tribes who catch the wicked.

As one reaches the center of the bridge, the whole
structure sways several feet to either side. One has the
feeling of being suspended above the rushing water. The
thin lacing of vines beneath one's feet free one of the law
of gravity, making it possible to hover or to move at will,
in space. There is no heaviness of heart or of tired feet
as one swings on a gossamer web while the damp air
whips one's hair, and the turbulent waters of rain-
drenched land roar beneath!

I stopped in the center of the bridge to enjoy the
swing of it, and to admire the spiderweb pattern of the
knotted lianas that made the net which held me, the pattern of the great cables that held the bridge to the trees
on either side of the river. On the far side, waiting to
cross when I was off the bridge, was an old, old Mano
woman. Around her neck were pounds of beads, and
glinting in the sun on the top strand, I saw my first Ag-

grey bead! There was no mistaking the Egyptian coloring of red and bright blue on a white core! Gone was all
thought of the wonder of the bridge in this greater wonder. The bridge became an uncertain support that I
must cross in great haste. My whole body trembled in
eagerness. My feet slipped through holes in the webbing.
I stumbled and turned my ankle and caught at the sides
and still I seemed no nearer to the prize ahead. Finally,
I reached the old lady.

'E-u-ah, Ma," I remembered to say. Even with an
Aggrey bead in front of one's eyes, one must not forget
the courtesy of greeting a native.

"E-u-ah, Ma," she returned my greeting, and brushed
her palms lightly against mine, and smiled.

I did not know enough Mano to ask for the bead, but
I pointed at it and offered the first coin I felt in my shirt
pocket, which happened to be a shilling. I made the
questioning gesture of exchange. She nodded, and broke
the raffia string that held the beads. Several worthless
ones fell into the river, but she caught the prized one in
her palm, while she clung to the broken ends of the bead
string with her other hand.

There it lay in the tan palm of her hand, which seemed
old enough to match the bead. Slowly the palm was extended toward me and I transferred it to my hand and
left the shilling in hers. I had in my possession one of the
things I had come to Africa to find!

The bead seemed identical with the one pictured in
Sir Harry Johnston's *Liberia,* one which was brought to
the British Isles by the Romans, and dredged up from
the mouth of the Thames. The same question came to

my mind which Sir Harry asks in his book, "Did the Aggrey beads of West Africa come across the Sahara and the Niger from Egypt or Carthage, or were they carried along the north coast of the Mediterranean from trading station to trading station, and so down the northwest and west coast of Africa?"

Had this bead which I held in my hand been made in Egypt or in Rome, and what route had it traveled through the centuries? If it could speak, it could answer unsolved questions about ancient Africa, about the origin and migration of tribes. Had it been carried on the vigorous wave of the Mohammedan conquest when it swept down over Africa? What tales it could tell of Guinea gold and pepper and slaves! How many times had it substituted for a human sacrifice in the rituals of the Poro Society? How many times had it purchased a strong slave's life? I felt guilty that for a shilling I had purchased the mute clue to so much that is not known. The history of centuries was contained in the colorful clay I clutched in my fist. The lacing of vines swayed and whirled and the cables that led to the trees crossed each other in front of my eyes, my knees gave way beneath me, and I sank to the floor of the bridge with the bead still grasped in my moist palm.

I saw in that moment the bead sacrifice of ancient Benin, the ceremony once a year when the keeper of the beads brought them all and set them before his king. Then a slave was brought and his head was "chocked" so that his blood ran over the beads. He then received instructions about what to tell the bead spirit whom he

was about to meet. Afterwards, he was led out and be-
headed, that he might in spirit form carry the message
that had been given him. The blood of slaves had probably trickled across the bead I held.

I climbed slowly off the bridge and watched the loads
come across one at a time. Some natives coming down
country waited to cross. They talked with old Saga while
they waited. Saga asked them if they had seen a motor
car.

"Ma, the man say that plenty rain spoil the bridge.
Motor car can't pass this side now-o."

Twenty miles to walk!

The road was the color of overfired pottery. It had
been baked by the kiln heat of the unshaded African
sun which beat at us with all its intensity as we hurried
down the road, straining our ears for the sound of a
motor. It is amazing how many of the jungle sounds of
birds and animals and branches scraping together re-
semble the panting of a Ford motor. Old Saga was not
fooled, but I was.

Finally we heard, unmistakably, the sound of a car.

"That one, the talk of a motorcar for true," Saga announced.

At the distance from which I saw him unfold from the
motorcar, Doctor Harley looked very tall. I think he
looked taller to me than he actually is because I knew
that his stature was that of a man who contained the
secrets of the people and of the forests.

When I shook his hand for the first time, it was the
handshake of strangers, a tentative acceptance implied.

Nothing of understanding was exchanged. Doctor Harley's glance is disturbingly penetrating. It seems to look through the surface aspects of things to the essential truth. Was I a joy-walking female journalist out to discover the bizarre which would be important to me only until it was written into a book that might sell? Did I really care about native lore? Did I sketch in a casual sort of pastime way, or was I serious and sincere? I could feel these questions back of the penetrating glance. I knew that the confidences of the natives were well guarded in Doctor Harley.

The carriers loaded the back of the pickup with all the cargo that could be piled on top or tied on the sides. The men were to sleep in the nearest village and walk on in the next day. Johnny came up to me with tears in his eyes.

"Missy," he said, "the day we leave you promise to keep me safe from the Mano Devil. If you leave me in the Mano town for the night, I don't think you can put eye on me again."

I looked at Doctor Harley and at the loaded pickup.

"Hang on to the front fender where it joins the motor-car," he said, and Johnny scuttled to the precarious perch.

After you have been walking at snail's pace for six days, twenty miles an hour seems a reckless and dangerous speed. At one place we went through a termite-eaten culvert, and were delayed over an hour getting out. The road was pitted with holes which the doctor skillfully dodged.

The sun was low when we finally drove up the mango-lined drive at Ganta Mission. The mangoes were great trees which Doctor had planted when the mission was first established.

Gene Harley was standing on the front steps, waving greeting, and Winifred came out of the door wearing a blue dress, looking exquisite. The blue of her dress and the black of her hair against the warm gray stones of the house were a perfect study in color. We went inside and sat beside a glowing fire that took away the chill of the evening. The flames cast warm shadows on the red wool country-cloth rug, and the mahogany paneling, and the bright-jacketed books on hand-made shelves. The warm glow that I felt was not all from the crackling fire; there was the warmth of welcome and happiness in the room. I knew an important thing — I had "found people."

We sat in the living room after dinner and talked to the accompaniment of a crackling fire. The mahogany paneling gleamed honey-colored in the light of the flames, as though the hot sun which had pulled the tree up through the darkness of the forest had left the golden dye of its strength in the veins of the wood.

We were interrupted by a sound like sand thrown against a window. No face nor shadow of body could be seen against the glass which caught only a faint glow of light from the fire. No one except myself seemed startled or surprised. Doctor got out of his chair and made his way without a light through the hall door. Winifred went on talking as though nothing had happened. When Doctor came back he held in his hand a brown bag of looped raffia. He went to the foot of the attic stairs.

"Would you like to come to see what I have?" he asked

me. "I don't know myself whether it is valuable or not.
I have to take these things sight-unseen in the dark."

I climbed the steps behind him, watching the stairs by
the swaying light of a lantern he carried. Each tread
emerged out of the darkness and was for a fleeting second
a secure oblong of lighted wood; then the lantern lifted
again, and greenish shadows leaped at the space where
the feet stood and swallowed them. The prickly tighten-
ing excitement, the drawn feel of my face that made it
seem rough though I had not touched it, brought me
back to childhood years when I had climbed alone to an
attic bedroom on cold winter nights, afraid of the enormous lantern-cast shadows, shaking partly with cold and
fear and partly with an ecstatic joy in the mobile flowing
forms of the dark images I could set in motion or command to be still with the yellow flame.

Doctor set the lantern and the raffia bag on a huge
chest. The light cast heavy ledges of shadow behind the
exposed rafters under the roof. There was the hot, closed-
up smell common to attics everywhere plus that inde-
scribable smell which those of us who live there call
"Africa smell." It fumes out of every closed case and
cupboard no matter how often they are sunned and
aired. It is something like the smell of a poorly fleshed
animal skin which has started to decompose and a little
like leaf mold after a rain in the forest, and much like
the sick-sweet smell of unembalmed dead. In my own
house the medicine case, the buffet drawers, the linen
closet, and even the bedding reeked of it. Here in the
attic where there were cases whose sacred contents could
not be taken into the sunlight without endangering the

lives of those who had made the acquisition possible, this
odor seemed to scent of Mystery. I was suffocating with
excitement. The deliberation with which Doctor folded
back the top of the bag was a thing I could hardly bear.
I could see only deep shadow in the depths of the sack.

Then he lifted up one of the shadows in his palm. It
was a smaller-than-life portrait mask of an old woman.
He moved it closer to the globe of the lantern while we
both looked and said nothing. Here in simple planes of
blackened wood was said all that could ever be said in
any medium — paint, or music, or words, or sculpture,
of the mellowing of age in quiet dignity through the
years.

Still without speaking, Doctor placed the mask in my
hands. I turned it to catch the light in different emphasis
on the features. I could see how she must have looked
before the cheeks were lined with character when she
danced with her age group at the coming-out of the Sande
bush. Then I saw the glint of morning sun on the high,
curved forehead as she leaned over a short-handled country hoe to tend the new rice she had planted. Her back
would have glistened like polished ebony with highlights
of raw umber on the curved muscles on either side the
shallow valley of the spine. These rippling highlights
would have seemed the reflections of the reddish earth
she tilled. The yellow-green spears of new growth were
moist with dew and wondrous in color against the black
and umber of her body, and the black hulk of charred
tree trunks lying crisscross where they fell when the jungle was brushed and fired to make the farm.

Then I lifted the chin of the mask to the light and saw

how she must have looked in the flickering leaf shadows in the forest when she carried white rice to the fertility altar and prayed to the ant-made phallus that she might become as productive as the field she had planted.

Year by year the lines of hard living had carved more deeply into her face, recording more of patience, and wistful yearning, of tenderness and wisdom. The carver had recorded this before the woman died, that her wisdom might live on and be seen in the medicine house of the tribe where it would be kept. The wonder of the mask and the beauty of it were part the skill of the carver and part the worth of her character. He had a great thing to say, and he had said it well.

I have seen portrait busts and portraits in oil which were considered "good likenesses," — which they may have been — but they were dead for all their fidelity to detail. Here was an extremely simple statement with almost no detail, in which the subject was vibrantly alive.

I gave the mask back to Doctor Harley. "I brought my carving chisels along," I said, "but now that I have seen this, I do not think that I can carve."

"I think I understand," he said gently. "I suggest you try clay for the present."

We went downstairs then. I felt very weary.

"We'll come back some other time and see the masks in the big cases," Doctor said. "I don't think you will want to look at any more tonight."

It must be this understanding of people's hearts which enables him to work such wondrous cures on their bodies, I thought. In the days that followed at Ganta, I saw this for a certainty.

CHAPTER NINETEEN

The Devil Walks

THE VOICE of the Devil, throaty and soft like breath blown across an empty bottle, floated down from the high hill beyond Ganta and roused me from sleep. A dream? No, there it was again, wooing and insistent. A sort of chord now, several voices calling together, huskily. It was plaintive like the mooing of a cow separated from her calf, but strong, too, and demanding.

"The voice of the Devil is sweet," Buno had told me once, "but it is cold air that leaves his mouth. It can make the back like the hard water in your ice machine." He had blown in his cupped palms to show me the sound of it. In Doctor Harley's attic, I had seen the black cylindrical clay pipes which are used to make the noise. They are small vases with pinched tops. There had been suppressed excitement among the houseboys that day, whispers about the Devil bush or Poro which was about to convene near Ganta for the first time in that generation.

Yes, the Devil blew a cold breath! I pulled up another blanket and went back to sleep. In the depths of the night I was awakened again by a sound hardly more warm than the blasts from the Devil's pipes. It was far away, part wail, part song, part deep lament. It was as though ghosts called out of their graves by the drums were trying their throats to regain earthly voices. The dog paced the porch and howled to the moon the way canines are supposed to do the night someone dies.

From the direction of the village, the treble of women's voices became distinguishable. The sound was tight and rasping, like the scraping of a high note on a violin string.

I fumbled for my clothes. In his room, Doctor Harley was pacing the floor. The crowd-sound gained in volume and eerie quality with the minutes. The Devil called again from the hills; the dog continued to howl. Moonlight flooded the yard with a viridian glow. A breeze flickered. It had the effect of a missile tossed into a shining pool. Waves of light broke against the leaves of the mangoes, the spines of the sisal, and the stirred spears of the palm fronds. When it had passed, each briefly liber–

ated leaf hung motionless again in the greenish light.
Only the measured tread of boots, and far away a wailing
crowd, were moving in the awful stillness. One felt the
bigness of the shadows under the trees, the bigness of the
black swamp beneath the hill, and the bigness of the
land. The stone house where we sat had seemed admir-
ably a part of the landscape until now. Suddenly, it
seemed alien to the land, isolated by the breath of the
Devil and the slowly approaching pagan rite. The age of
the stone mission house was as nothing compared to the
stone altars of the forest. I knew why Doctor Harley's
feet could not be still while the Devil walked.

He came out on the porch.

"Do you want to go with me?" he asked. His voice was
weary and suffering.

We followed our ears to a procession. Leading it were
men beating drums, reeling forward in circles as they
played. After them came the boys of the village wearing
nothing but breechcloths. They did not dance but
moved like sleepwalkers. Behind them came the mothers
and all the women of the village. They were almost
naked except for trailing vines cascading down their
writhing bodies. Some old, shriveled crones who could
not walk without sticks leaned on clubs and gyrated
around them. The more vigorous women were twisting,
leaping, and jerking to the rhythm of the drums. Their
faces held rigid expressions that spoke of both ecstasy
and pain. Their throats were loose now, with an old
grief too worn by reiteration to hold the sobs tight any
longer. There was something of a fanged snarl in it like
a she-animal defending her cubs. It told of the piercing

agony of childbirth. I had heard this sound in the huts behind my house when a child could not be born readily and the old women whipped the woman's abdomen with bamboo rods to persuade the child to leave the security of the womb.

As the women danced and contorted their bodies, they flopped their pendulous breasts, wafer-thin now and vestigial, to their faces and kissed the empty flaps over and over, as though aware of the blessedness of having given suck to children who were about to become men. Their tears mingled with the slobberings of saliva and the coarse nipples shone in the moonglow.

I do not pretend to be able to "think black." Cutting new thought channels is slow and tortuous like a river's sawing through the soil to establish a new bed. I think that Doctor Harley has suffered this to be accomplished in himself during his twenty-five years of Ganta so that he can come inside the natives' way of thinking. He is the only person I have ever met of whom I believe this to be true. But although I cannot think in the native woman's way, I was born to the soil, though in a different land, and I was born female. When I saw these women weltering in the agony of giving birth, tossing and pitching under the fruiting vines they wore, I think I understood in a small way why there were tears on their breasts. In our civilization, the pangs that go with seeing a child become a man are spread out over many years. There is the poignancy of the morning a woman waves to her child on his way to his first day of school, her wistfulness when she buys his first pair of long trousers, the tears she sheds the day he is married. In Liberia this is all com-

pacted into a few hours of one night. Until a boy goes
to the Poro, he is without a soul, without even the name
he will have later. Then, suddenly, one night she goes
with him as far as the mat wall around the sacred grove.
Inside he will suffer. If he lives to come out, he will
emerge a *man*. As they danced their way down the road
there must have been in the eyes of all of them the image
of a fragment of clay pot that would be left before the
doors of some of their huts, a token that a son had died
in the Poro. None could say he was dead nor mourn him,
but he would not be seen again. On the day when the
others came out of the Bush, their new raised welts of
skin designs still a little raw, some would not be there to
wear the new country cloth the weavers had made for
the glad day.

The moon was incandescent on the sacred hill, holding it like the beam of a torch, and the procession traveled in its direction. When all the people had passed, we
joined the rear of the group unnoticed. The soles of my
booted feet ached unbearably. The drums vibrating
through the earth must have shocked the bare feet of the
dancers into an almost painful response that was un-
studied, automatic, elemental. The tingling in my own
feet was not so much a desire to dance as an ache that had
its origin in the thumped air inside the skin-covered hollow logs. It was a torture like being beaten on the bot-
toms of the feet with rods.

An old man with a cow's tail wand-encased in a leather
handle stopped the crowd at frequent intervals, seem-
ingly to impress them with the sacredness of the progress.
While the wand was held aloft the boys stood mute and

statue-still while the women danced in place. They were getting closer to the spot where the boys would "die to the world" and be reborn as men out of the maw of the Devil.

When light shafted over the eastern hills we left the group and started back slowly to the mission house. I could not ask Doctor Harley to talk then, but later I read a description in his *Notes on the Poro* [1] of what happens to the boys when they reach the wall of the grove. Each boy apparently would be impaled on a spear and thrown over a raffia curtain which marked the entrance to the Devil's domain. Actually the spear would pass through a banana stalk that had been lashed to his torso, under a cloak of country cloth. The spear would also pierce an animal bladder filled with blood, making his "death" realistic to the watching audience, even to the thud when his body hit the ground on the other side of the curtain.

Breakfast at the mission was a quiet meal except for some conversation with Fau, the steward boy.

"Dottar," said Fau, shifting from one of his huge bare feet to the other, "I am a small boy." Fau was the largest native boy I had seen, and much larger than any of us.

Doctor's sense of humor had not been drowned in the deep sorrow he felt that the God of Love was encompassed by the gods of frightfulness.

"You are a small mountain, Fau," he said.

Fau walked to the end of the dining room so that he could face all of us. When he moved he seemed to propel

[1] George W. Harley, *Notes on the Poro in Liberia*. Published by the Peabody Museum, Harvard University.

himself forward by halves with the leverage of his huge legs. He crossed his arms.

"Dottar," he repeated, "I am a small boy. I want to go to the Devil bush to become a man."

"But you are a civilized boy, Fau," Doctor said. "We have taken much care to teach you."

"Dottar," he said miserably, "look at my foot."

We all looked at the mound of flesh which composed this enormous extremity.

"All right," Fau went on, "suppose I take a cutlass and cut off the big toe? Can that toe walk alone?" This was a purely rhetorical question and he did not pause for an answer. "I am a *person* only as I am a member of my tribe. I can no more walk alone than my toe can walk if I cut him off. If I do not get the Devil's toothmarks on my back, I do not belong to my people. I am as dead to them, less than a dead goat. For a goat that is dead is a dead goat. I would be dead to them without ever having been anything."

Embarrassed at having spoken so strongly to the Doctor who had done so many things for him, Fau's eyes spurted tears, and he lumbered blindly out of the room. The next stack of corn cakes were brought in by Sendro the cook. We did not see Fau again that day or after.

"Fau has gone to let the Devil eat him," Sendro said. "And Qua-Qoi also!"

Winifred's busy household was left without any help except old Sendro smoking his clay pipe over the hot kitchen stove. As is the way with her, she spoke more about the implications of the situation for the boys than of her own inconvenience. I thought that my Johnny who had been doing nothing but show off his fine uniforms might come to the rescue. I found him in the kitchen hall, crouched into a sodden bundle of weeping humanity. He was doubled up with his head between his knees; a sort of ostrich psychology, I thought. If the minions of the Mano Devil were abroad looking for Bassau boys for the ceremony of opening the Poro, at least he would not see them. I spoke to him and shook him, but he did not hear me and seemed not to recognize me. His eyes and ears were plugged with terror. Through the long day he stayed there. Toward evening he roused and made a pretense of cleaning my room.

"Missy, I beg you," he croaked in a voice hoarse with weeping, "let me sleep across the door of your room tonight."

At dusk the crowd-sound came again, weary and muted. Tired old women lurched along the trail toward their village, the dust thick around their ankles. The vines and flowers in their hair were wilted and gray. Their bodies were slack with fatigue, as wilted as their garlands. Some of them sobbed softly like children who have gone to sleep crying. On to the village. There was much work to be done, much thread to be spun against the day of Resurrection when the youth who had died before their eyes would come again, ready to "take cloth" and live as men of the Manos.

CHAPTER TWENTY

Ganta in Action

Gᴀɴᴛᴀ was a place of increasing amazement and reward. How so few people managed to do so many things is a mystery. There is a dispensary where hundreds of people are treated daily. Some of them come in hammocks suspended from poles carried on the shoulders of two relatives. Their journey is often entirely across the country. There is a sick village where the hordes live during their treatment. There is a leper colony where several hundred lepers have their own chief, their own industries and rice fields. The schoolhouse is a beautiful two-story building of gray gneiss topped with red tile. The schoolboys live in a colony of native houses and wear country cloth because care is taken that they do not grow away from their own people nor learn to despise native ways. Add to this a power sawmill, a blacksmith's shop, a furniture factory, a kiln, a swimming pool, a demonstration farm in a drained swamp, and a tile plant and you have part of the picture. In addition to keeping all of these activities at full hum, Winifred Harley has done the Liberian collection of plants for

Kew Gardens, and Doctor has done the Liberian Collection for the Peabody Museum, written two books, and made the only map of the country which is in any way accurate.

Once when I asked Doctor what he intended to do next, he answered, "Three things." Yet he speaks and walks slowly and there is no flurry anywhere. There was always time to explain anything I asked about, time to go into the attic and explain every mask and piece of carving, time to teach me how to temper steel, and time to make a workbench for me in the carpenter shop.

When I said I would like to do wood engraving of native wood, if I had the wood and the tools, he said, "We'll find the wood, and I'll make the tools, if you really want to do it. I have always wanted to see this country illustrated in block prints." Eventually he had to take a sill out of the sawmill to get wood that was hard enough and properly cured. The engraving tools he made from the tooth of an old hayrake, a spike of good steel he had carried all the way from Carolina. As he forged them, he told me about his father who was a blacksmith, and how knowing this work had been the wedge with which he first entered the confidence of the natives.

One day as I walked toward the leper colony, two lepers stepped out of the bushes where they were concealed. In the hand of each was his personal *me*, or small portrait mask idol. These may not usually be seen by another native, let alone a white person. I reached down to take the masks and saw that the palms which held them had no fingers. Then I looked at their feet and saw that their toes were gone.

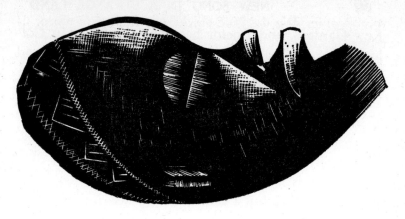

The masks were beautiful and I was delighted to have them offered to me.

"How is it," I said, "that you allow me to put eye on these? Are they not sacred to you?"

One of them scuffed the stump which had once been a foot into the dust.

"Ma," he said, "for many moons and many rice-plantings, we pray to these. Every new moon we kill white chicken and feed the blood to the mask. We pray to make the sickness stop eating us. One toe dies and drops away. All right! We bring more blood, make more pray. Another toe dies and is dead meat for the dogs. Then we come to this white medicine man with the strong medicine of the white God. By this time all the toes and all the fingers are gone and the blood runs where we walk. The white man puts his strong medicine in a needle and no more pieces of us fall down like nuts from the tree. Skin closes over the blood. So we say it must be that the God of the Strong Medicine is strong past the gods of our people. We do' give chicken to these any more. If you like, we take them."

I took them gladly!

Doctor Harley has never committed the crime of which many missionaries are guilty — asking the natives to burn their gods. He is too much of an anthropologist and too much of an artist. His big collection has come to him voluntarily by people who have no further use for their fetishes. It is not the purpose of this book to comment on mission work but I cannot help postscripting it with the remark that I wish all missionaries were anthropologists and medical doctors. Those who feel that Christianity and Western civilization are synonymous have wreaked unmeasured havoc. When all the old ideas are destroyed before new ones have had time to grow into a way of living, there is chaos and tragedy.

The superficial quality of the quick-change teachings of some groups was shown by a native boy who once came to my house on the plantation. I noticed that his arm had been tattooed with a strange head, quite unlike any native drawings or the usual geometric tattoo.

"It's Jesus," the boy told me.

"But why?" I asked.

"Well, Ma," he said. "I go to one mission school. I sit down there. The missionary tell me I got to get Jesus under my skin. Then I can't do bad thing again. So I get photo of Jesus from one English book and I have him put under my skin."

"And does that stay your bad ways?" I asked.

"No, Ma," he said. "It don't. And it hurt like hell!"

Doctor Harley's way is to first understand the native

idea of death and resurrection as it is portrayed in the Poro. On this basis he can build into the Mano mind a meaningful Christ story.

The big event of the week for the natives in the Ganta community is market.

Yellow headcloths dipped in turmeric, indigo lappas patterned in white with cassava batiking, creamy white tunic shirts of country cloth reaching to men's knees, the gleaming tooth-white heaps of rice, red-violet colo nuts against fresh yellow-green leaves lining the panniers, the blue purple of eggplants, the fuzzy green of okra, the tans and browns of baskets and mats, the flash of brass and copper jewelry, the glistening brown black of dark skin — these are the colors that carpet the swept earth of the village compound.

By two o'clock everyone had found a place to sit and had spread his wares on a bamboo mat, but no exchange of goods could take place until the market was officially opened. Ringing bells and tooting horns, the market soldiers, who had been accumulating gusto by drinking large quantities of palm wine on the piazza of the chief's house, cleared a path through the crowd. The chief followed them, surveying people and produce. His long blue-and-white-striped robe trailed over the baskets and calabashes as he passed. He mounted a termite mound and held aloft a cow's-tail wand. There was a silence so absolute that the flickering wing of a caged chicken was conspicuous. The market master made a speech setting forth the price ceilings for the day. Any infringement on the local OPA would be severely punished. With this point clarified in vehement language, the soldiers went through the crowd collecting two cents bounty for the chief from each seller. The chief dropped his wand. Normally the buying and selling would begin with a great shout of "Aiiii-o!" and a surge of the crowd, but this day there was a special feature. A boy who had been to the coast and learned "civilized ways" (so theft is considered) had stolen a small piece of country cloth from a Ganta woman. He was to be beaten before the crowd.

Everyone waited quietly, stretching his neck to get a better view of the boy who was led forth from one of the huts. He walked haughtily erect. A few people quietly shifted their positions to get a better view. The boy went straight to the only tree in the compound and faced the trunk. The khaki-clad soldier who was to administer the flogging rolled up his sleeves and flexed his biceps for all to admire. He flourished the whip so that all might see it was sturdily made of rawhide and had many tails with a knot on the end of each tail. The crowd nodded. The soldier was strong and the flail well made. Good! The boy was shifted a bit so that his back was in full view of more people. The chief gave the signal. The soldier grasped the whip with both hands after spitting in his palms. The whip was drawn far back. A swish as it cuts the air and a dull thud as it lands on the boy's back! He recoiled from the blow, steadied himself on the tree. No blood, yet. The crowd counted the strokes aloud, some in Mano, some in Mandingo, the soldiers in English. Two! A little blood oozed that time; the soldier had found his strength. Never had I known that twenty-five could be so far from one! When the last blow fell, the boy slumped into a heap at the base of the tree, and his back looked like pounded steak. Still the crowd waited. Could he walk? Yes, he was on one knee, trying to stand. Stumbling a little at first, he made his way back to the hut with unbowed head. No one attended him nor spoke to him. The ways of the coast must be purged. Now the market could begin.

I made my way to the edge of the crowd where some tall Mandingos had strung lengths of country cloth on a raffia clothesline. I was most interested not in the cloth on the line, but in the handsomely embroidered burnooses which they wore. The bargaining was something like this:

MYSELF (feeling the texture of the white cloth appreciatively): "Oh, Pa, the robe you wear is fine."

MANDINGO (smiling so all his facial muscles pointed up toward his red fez): "Thank you, Ma."

Some five minutes are consumed while I admire the design of the stitchery, the workmanship, the dazzling cleanliness and finally lead up to the idea that I would like to buy it. In hundreds of cases this was the end of the deal; I had never persuaded a Mandingo to sell his robe. I kept on trying in what seemed the futile hope that some day I would get one. To my surprise, on this day, the old man seemed slightly interested.

MANDINGO: "How much you fit to pay?"

MYSELF: "How much you can ask, Pa?"

MANDINGO: "Three pounds, Ma, will take him off my back."

MYSELF: "Oh, Pa! How can you talk so?"

MANDINGO: "All right, how much you give? Remember I am your pa with the good heart of a father to you, and the robe, fine."

MYSELF: "One pound can leave my hand."

MANDINGO (with crocodile tears): "And I thought you were as a daughter to me. Oh, the sadness in my heart!"

A crowd gathers around us and the bargaining goes on for more than an hour, the Mandingo gradually working down, and myself working upward toward the compromise of one pound, ten. Each of us has made the same concessions so neither of us has lost face, and we have reached the price we each had in mind in the beginning.

MANDINGO: "All right! The bargain finish. But how can I take off my coat before the people?" (He would have had at least three voluminous layers beneath, including trousers which bagged in the dust.)

MYSELF: "Go then to your house, Pa. Certainly you have more coats inside, for you are a rich man."

The Mandingo trotted off to his house and emerged again with the robe I had bought. He was wearing a more beautifully embroidered one than the one he had sold. The bargaining began anew. I bought three robes from him, and when he came out of his house the last time, he was in tatters.

After I left Ganta, my pa was kneeling on a mat saying his prayers in his last robe. A hawk swooped low for some chickens who were also occupying the mat and became tangled in the frayed ends of the garment. Pa stopped praying long enough to catch the hawk in his hands. Thus did Allah bless the old man with hawk soup for the bargaining away of all of his presentable coats.

Johnny tagged along after me with the three robes in a bundle on his head while I started to search for old beads and bracelets and leopard teeth. The crowd who had watched the trading of the burnooses followed us with interest, and the rice sales began to suffer. Aluminum hairpins made like ornamental hatpins came out of old mommie's hair and were thrust at me eagerly. Bracelets came off arms and legs. Beads were taken from necks and torsos and held under my nose. I began to suspect that I had paid too much for the robes.

Many of the beads were worthless junk imported by the Syrian traders at the coast. Others were identical to Czechoslovakian beads I had seen in ten-cent stores in the United States. A few were the old, old ones I wanted.

Among the leopard teeth offered to me was one which was almost but not quite convincing. The shape was right, the coloring was correct, even to the discoloration where the tooth enters the jaw socket, but something about the light on the edges aroused my suspicion that this tooth had never been inside a leopard's mouth. I took it between my thumbs and it broke like a drinking glass!

"Where did you get this?" I asked.

The boy and all the crowd broke into a gleeful roar.

"Before the big war," said the boy, "the Japanese people sent these in a boat to Monrovia."

"Well," I said, "I have broken it and I will pay you for it. It's a prize example of the lowest thing I have ever seen in imitation."

"Well," he admitted, "it is true that it does not carry much medicine for being strong like a leopard."

I paused before a Mandingo girl who wore a gorgeous gold filligree ornament at her neck. The gold had been made into a wire, fine as spiderwebbing and twisted into intricate design. It was cubical and about the size of an artgum eraser.

"Would you like to sell your ornament?" I asked her.

Her eyes lighted with an animal fire. There was a snakelike hiss in her throat. She glared at me with cold contempt while she gathered saliva in her mouth, and spat full against the side of my face. My first reaction was rather uncomplicated amazement. All the others had been so eager to bargain, had seemed to think it was great fun.

Amazement subsided. Admiration for her pride took its place. I do not think there was any turn-the-other-cheek humility in what I felt, but rather something of pride in her pride, the kind of thing one feels toward a spirited unbroken colt. Perhaps another reason I felt no anger was that I did not think her venom was discharged at me personally as much as toward the whole race of

white Christian women I represented. I was but one of
them and at that moment I had no particular urge to de-
fend them. I wore boots and trousers and strode across
the country, free as a man, bearing no burdens, tending
no rice, chopping no wood, cooking no food. Further-
more, I had a chance of earning the Christian heaven in
my own right, a place where no tasks have been described
more arduous than twanging a harp. If she ever got to
the Mohammedan heaven, it would be as one of the
large and bright-eyed maidens whom "no man nor jinni
had followed before," kept in tents beside the Gardens of
Pleasure, attending the lusts of worthy males reclining
on gold-weft couches, men whose strength of back and
appetite was guaranteed in writing by Allah through his
true Prophet. All the gold weft she would ever know
was on this earth where she could wear a cube of it at
her neck. Now I wanted to take even this from her!

Johnny reached for the immaculate handkerchief he
always kept folded in fancy design in his breast pocket,
and dabbed it against my wet cheek. In his eyes was as
much compassion as though it were blood from a wound
he sopped, staining the white folds. The chief, who had
seen these events, swore a strenuous oath and hurried
toward me with his soldiers at his heels. The crowd
waited breathlessly.

"This woman is big with pride," he boomed. "Let her
grow small under the twenty-five [lashes]. Let the woman
who hates you be without children. Let —— "

"No," I stopped him. "That is not my wish. Tell the
woman that I salute her spirit."

The woman went on with her market work, counting

out little piles of okra, three to a pile, and arranging them in a design on a mat.

The chief spoke to her in a blazing voice and what he said was most certainly not what I had asked him to tell her. The crowd roared approval. She paid no more attention to him than she did to me, and with outward calm completed the design of the okra. When the chief finished the tirade, he flicked the end of her nose with his wand, and she brushed at it as though it were nothing more than a bothersome fly.

I talked with my carriers as I walked from the market. The robes and beads and other things I had purchased bobbed along on their heads, and their voices sounded muffled under the loose-wrapped burdens.

"If the Mandingo traders sold pride, of which they have plenty, with their salt and cola and cloth, and calabashes that they carry up and down West Africa," I said, "you natives could be free of the Liberians. You never saw a Mandingo stand under the hammock of a government man and run all day without rest or food."

"That is true, Missy," said Johnny. "But suppose the Mandingos sold the machine for washing clothes and the machine for cutting grain that you have in your country. Our people would not know how to use these things. They would still carry their dirty clothes to the waterside. They would still cut the rice, one stem, one stem, with a small knife. If the Mandingos sold pride, it would be the same way. Pride would make us free, but we would not know what to do with free."

It was a great truth he spoke. Freedom, like the Christian God, needs to come gradually to the forests.

CHAPTER TWENTY-ONE

Down Country

I HAD LIVED in the interior for almost two months and it was time to start down country.

"What if the headman can't get carriers?" I asked Doctor Harley. It's a helpless feeling to want to move and to know that one can't go a step unless enough natives agree to carry the loads.

"Oh, I think Sendro can find men."

"But if he doesn't?"

"The District Commissioner can always send soldiers to catch men, if necessary."

I didn't want to travel with forced labor. I went to the kitchen to talk with Sendro.

"Sendro!"

"Yeah, Ma?"

"What time you can find carriers? I want to send paper to Firestone. What time I can tell my man come for end of the motor road to carry me?"

"Well, Ma, I can't say. Carrier palaver be hard-o this time. Plenty men go for Devil bush. Saga, self, go for Devil bush."

"You try for me, yah, Sendro?"

"Oh, Ma, I try like hell-o."

"But what day we can start?"

"Well, Ma, I can't say."

They do well in Africa who learn to sit and wait.

Market day came, and market day again, before Sendro had accumulated enough indifferent clansmen to carry my loads.

"It isn't as though I needed hammock men," I told Doctor. That means twelve less men than the usual safari.

"You're riding in a hammock this time, young lady. And you're going to stay in it."

"But I hate hammocks. They make my stomach sick. I can walk as well as a native. Why must they carry me?"

"I've got good medical reasons, and it's orders."

"Well, Sendro, we start today, yah?" Ten days had passed.

"Ma, I want to tell you something." Sendro shifted from foot to foot.

"What thing you say, Sendro?"

"Ma, the men say they must go market today to buy rice. No rice on the road this time, Ma."

"Oh, all right. But tomorrow time, soon morning, before chicken talk, we go, yah? You try for me, Sendro!"

"Oh, Ma, I try."

Winifred and Doctor had both insisted that Sendro go down country with me.

"But what will you do for a cook?" I objected. "With Fau and your second steward off to the Poro bush, you will be left without any houseboys. I can't agree."

"Sendro will go," Doctor said with finality. "He is absolutely reliable and with Saga off in the Devil bush there is no one else for whom the men have much respect. Sendro is a big man in the Poro Society and the men all do what he tells them. The carriers will be a bad lot and you'll need a good head man to keep them on the trail."

The day after, Ganta market came again. I looked out of the window expecting to see twenty nondescript men arguing about which head load each of them would carry. The lawn was bare of people except for three old women who were waiting to sell cocoa pods to Winifred. I went to the kitchen to find Sendro.

"Ma, we can't put foot to the trail today. I be big man for the Society. Today is the day it is necessary for me to do my-part palaver in the Society for my country brother. Tomorrow I come again and we go for true."

Sendro came back from the sacred grove after three days. He brought bad news.

"We cannot put eye on Saga again," he said.

"You mean it was necessary for Saga to die in the Poro bush?"

"Ma, we cannot put eye on Saga again." He would say no more about it.

The carriers came at last. Doctor Harley drove me to the Devil bridge across the St. John. The time had come to say good-bye to the busy man who had given so much of his time to help me accomplish my ends. We snapped fingers; it seemed the appropriate way.

"Thank you — for everything!" Only the *everything* made it adequate in the least. I might have lived in

Africa for many years without discovering the native lore I had learned in a few weeks with his help.

I sat down on some cases and waited for the carriers for whom there had been no room in the pickup.

Sendro busily strung a hammock from a couple of trees.

"Sendro!"

"Yeah, Ma?"

"How you fit to lift hammock? You think we sleep here, this place? We sleep tonight far down the trail."

"It good for Ma to rest. We can no put eye on carriers for long time."

Obediently I climbed into the hammock. Sendro covered me with a blanket. I pulled it over my head to keep off the tsetse flies and sweltered to sleep. The sun stood overhead when Sendro roused me.

"Let go, Ma."

"Where the men?"

"All go before, Ma."

"But the water? I want to drink."

"Here, Ma." He handed me the canteen and rolled the hammock.

Ha, I thought, the hammock frame is in front. Good! I won't have to argue with Sendro. But I was wrong. When I had weaved across the Devil bridge and passed through the town, the hammock men were waiting with the hammock frame on their heads, dancing and singing.

"I wait, small, for ride hammock, Sendro. I walk the bad ground here. Hammock too rough," I started to descend a steep gulch. Sendro dug his crooked toes into the rough gravel so it couldn't roll under his feet and braced himself before each step while I hung onto his wrist. He looked sad. It would not be easy to keep the ma in the hammock and Doctor had told him he must see to it.

Sendro smoked a short clay pipe with a big hunk of glowing charcoal on it. He seemed to be carrying a bonfire just under his little button nose. His voice was big and bass. It always startled me when it exploded out of his small frail body. His idea of managing a trek was to run back and forth along the path beside the carriers waving his cow's-tail wand and yelling, *"Allez! Allez!"* The slow ones got flicked with the cow's tail. One old man had trouble keeping the pace and often felt the side of Sendro's gnarly foot applied to what would have been the seat of his trousers, had he been wearing any. Whenever one of the men had to stop to relieve himself, the whole procession was commanded to stop so it would not get out of order. No one was allowed to step off the trail. Encouragement and advice were freely given to the one who had occasioned the halt. The necessity was a contagious idea.

"Sendro!"

"Yeah, Ma?"

"Missy go for bush, small."

Sendro looked at me reproachfully. A headman has many troubles.

Although much time had been wasted in starting on the march, I wanted to stop for a while at the village of Chief Nya Qua. I had heard that among the chief's many wives were old women with ancient beads.

As we approached the town, Sendro said, "Get in the

hammock, Ma. We come to the town just now. If Ma no ride in the hammock it be a shame palaver."

I sat in the hammock. Sendro adjusted a pillow at my back.

The carriers were like spirited horses spoiling for a work-out. They pranced and whirled the hammock in circles which carried us slowly forward down the path. They sang about me in Mano. A leader led out with my country name, Kau Blouzio, which means first-born woman of her mother who can stand on her own feet. They said it meant more than the ability to walk, and told me fables to show it meant independence and self-reliance.

"Kau Blouzio, Kau Blouzio, Kau Blouzio!
The woman that God fashioned like the trunk of tall tree,
The woman that moves like a field of rice before the wind,
The ma with the medicine for shoot the meat,
The long ma, the swift ma, our ma who walks with we."

Then all the carriers took up the chorus of "Kau Blouzio! Ho! Kau Blouzio! Ho!" giving the leader time to compose additional eulogies.

The carriers whirled me up to the piazza of Nya Qua's chief-house in a cloud of dust and noise.

Nya Qua sat in a tasseled hammock of purple raffia. Under his bright red fez his face was lean and tense with crafty intelligence. The perspiration that shone on his brow seemed the sweat of his thinking. He wore a voluminous blue-and-white-striped chief-robe and red Mandingo slippers. Seated on the floor all about him were more than thirty of his wives spinning cotton thread with little clay tops. He rose to greet me but I could not get out of the hammock until the carriers finished their mad dance. It was like being thrown in a blanket. I was jolted and bounced until I was seasick and choked with dust. The song leader had saved his most elaborate praises to sing before the chief:

"The hair of the ma is black and long like the vines that climb to the
 top of the high bush;
The eye of the ma is bright like the lightning that strikes the tall tree;
The hand of the ma can make photo in clay;
The gun of the ma can make the meat in the bush to die of fear
 far away;
The big woman is ma to we, the big woman got good heart for **we.**
Kau Blouzio! Ho! Kau Blouzio! Ho! HO! HO!"

With a final "Ho!" that almost pitched me out of the hammock, the dancing and singing stopped and I staggered dizzily toward the chief. We snapped fingers until my joints seemed dismembered.

"*E-u-ah*, Pa!"

"*E-u-ah*, Ma!"

This went on for some time, each of us repeating the greeting with increasing gusto until it threatened to become an endurance contest. Perhaps it was native courtesy for me to change the subject. Nya Qua spoke both Mano and Kpuesi, so in desperation I gave him the Kpuesi greeting.

"*Ba-tu-ah*, Pa!"

This was too much for Nya. Orange cola juice ran down the corners of his mouth and like a garden hose, he spat a stream of amber before he collapsed in his hammock with laughter.

"*Ba-tu-ah*, aye!" The wives took it up like a chant,

and the headwife led me to a hammock beside Nya's purple one.

The orchestra arrived then, a dozen small boys with drums and wooden horns. The horns were elongated and twisted cone shapes, with holes near the small ends into which the boys blew with puffed-out cheeks. They muted them by sticking their fists into the large ends. The drums thumped with strident vitality. The horns cracked the air. They were the whistle of the wind that twists the strong arms of the trees in a jungle storm; softening again into the fluttering of the blue-tailed veda bird dancing on the air with spread feathers before its drab mate; enlarging now into the shriek of the mourn-

ers at a big man's funeral wake; lifted and stretched into a thin wail, crystal clear as a thread of boiling sugar syrup before it breaks and falls again into the seething bubbling molten mass from which it was lifted. Scattered now like chipped ice by the chubby fists rammed into the ends of the twisted wooden funnels.

The players flowed together when they had finished and made a circle, the rim of which was patterned evenly by the dent of shining brown buttocks thrust out that their heads might be close for whispered conference.

"Sendro, tell the chief that the music is fine, that it takes the tired from my feet."

The orchestra assembled and began to play again. Nya kicked off his slippers, took a hasty bite of cola nut, and ran out in the sun-drenched compound to dance. His robe stood out in a right angle to his body as he spun, crouched, rose again, turning rapidly all the time.

He was a spinning top flicked into faster and ever faster rotations by the sting of the drums, a whirlpool in a rain-swollen stream, an eddy of fallen leaves whipped from their branches by a rain-lashed gale, a bush cow stalking the hunter in narrowing circles, hurtling his weight forward on frenzied dainty feet, and finally a tired old man, dripping perspiration and slobbering cola juice on discolored lips. He staggered to the piazza step and leaned against the smooth porch post and was silent. The horns were silent, too, but the drums fluttered on like the echo of a desperately palpitating heart. I thought that should they stop sharply, the rasped and heaved breathing of the old man would cease with a final and terrible shudder. One of the wives fanned him with a palm frond and another brought him a fresh cola, which he nibbled greedily.

When he was able to speak he asked Sendro to tell me that now I must dance some dance of my people. It was impossible to refuse, but what could I do? Everyone looked at me expectantly while my mind pictured and rejected the poor spectacle I would make doing any of the dances that I knew.

"Do the one I see you do at the club, Missio. This one —— " Johnny did a few jittering steps, and the drums felt for the rhythm of it.

"I can't do that one, one person alone, Johnny."

"I know that dance, Missy. Every night you dance at the club, I watch your feet the whole time. I can help you show the people the United States dance. You touch my hand so, you go from me like you vex, you come back this side like fit to beat me, but no, you spin under your arm like you say, 'I finish with this foolish thing,' but all the time you act vex, then say you glad."

Johnny did indeed know the dance, and the music was right. I took my cues from Johnny who got in a lot of fancy footwork while he danced almost in one spot flinging me forward and back and around with his strong little fingers gripped into the cup of my hand. The Kpuesi and Mano equivalents of "bravo" almost drowned out the orchestra. The players, not to be surpassed in volume of sound, pounded the drums until I thought that the tight-stretched monkey skins would split and the ballooned cheeks of the horn players burst. I saw them in a wavy blur that came into view, focused slightly, and receded before I was whirled to face them again.

When we had finished, it was the drums which stopped suddenly. The horns subsided into soft gusts as hot breath was sucked and released through them.

"The chief say," announced Sendro whose nose glowed with pride and the heat of his clay pipe, "that the civilized dance is a fine thing."

Civilized? We wouldn't go into that.

"Tell the chief, Sendro, that the best drum music in my country has for its ma the drums of this country."

Nya looked pleased. He spoke long to Sendro with many gestures.

"The chief tell me just now, Ma, that he like plenty civilized thing. He like to know all the civilized ways. He like to have a motorcar and he like to know how many wives he must sell to buy one motorcar. He like one car the same color his hat."

"Ask the chief how he would manage with a motorcar when there are no roads."

"He say, Ma, he will let it live in the compound and he will sit in his hammock the whole day and look at the fine thing. But it is not the motorcar only that the chief like. He want to learn plenty civilized thing. He beg the ma to sit down here many days and show him plenty new ways."

I was concerned about this longing for the tinsel of civilization. I had seen the straightforwardness of many boys from the bush turn into whining sycophancy when they came to the coast. A native man met on the trail does not have to adjust his demeanor before he greets you. Even if he wears some clothing he does not re-arrange it nervously. He *is,* he does not have to seem to be. His eye meets yours, neither asking from you nor giving to you anything but the greetings of the trail. If he leaves the trail behind and exchanges the rice he has carried on his head for a sun helmet, he cannot look at you in the old way from beneath the brim. The eyes learn to hold contempt and anger, resentful of what has been lost, and covetous of what cannot be attained. It is not the cold and noble hate of the cleanly robbed, but the bewildered gizzard-sand irritation of the frustrated. The helmet is the beginning of an unending mountain of things which he desires. The desire sandpapers his soul with unrest, he begs or steals or cheats to assuage for a little with getting, until another want has taken its place. Finally, diseased with wants he cannot attain, and discredited, the security of the communal tribe lost to him, he must think of new chicanery or starve.

If only I could speak to the chief about the goodness of native ways! But I did not know enough of his languages, and he did not know mine. I remembered a story Poor Boy had told me one afternoon while I sewed and ironed in the laundry room.

"Sendro, ask the chief if he would like to give ear to a story the Bassau people tell about civilized ways. Buno knows the story and can tell it in Kpuesi."

The chief would like very much to hear the story. Johnny had held the center of the stage with his dancing. Now, although the story came from the Bassaus, a Kpuesi boy was to have his turn at being the focus of attention. The wives gathered in the compound with the carriers and the orchestra. Nya's hammock and mine were moved from the piazza and tied between breadfruit trees.

Buno sat on the swept clay in the center of the group, with the sunlight beating down on his head. After a long pause during which Nya ate more cola, he began. Buno's back was well-marked with the raised scars of the Kpuesi Devil; he came from a noble father. It was right that even an old chief with many wives should listen when the young son of the Sanoyea blacksmith spoke.

"Once some people had a fine daughter in the Sande [the tribal devil school held in the sacred grove and comparable to the Poro for the boys]."

Buno's voice was bright with youth. It rose and fell in the tonal Kpuesi syllables like music. No one stirred.

"While the girl learned the plenty thing that women-part must know, the ma worked hard against the day the girl would come from the bush and take cloth." (Pagan girls usually wear only hip beads until they emerge from the Sande, when they start to wear a lappa.)

"The girl's people grow fine cotton, the ma roll all the seeds out, and make it grow big belly on the bow [the system of flipping it around the string on a hunting bow to card it]. While she work she say, 'When my daughter come from the bush, she will marry the chief, and grow big belly like the cotton and have plenty man-pickin for the chief.' While the ma work and make the cotton grow big, a hornbill fly down to the palaver house with a big noise, *Br-r-r!* He flap his wings so [elbows beaten in and out] and say in a loud voice, 'So it will be, for true.' And the woman glad.

"Then the woman spin the cotton into thread with a fine top made from sacred clay, and she say, 'So will move the feet of my daughter when she come from the bush and dance for all the people to see.' Again the hornbill fly to the palaver house and say, 'You speak true. So it will be.'

"Then the ma dye the thread and make it a bright sun-color with the root of turmeric. And the woman say, 'So will be the smile of the girl pickin I have born, and so will be the gold of the rice she will plant in the fields.' And the hornbill came again and said, 'So it will be if the girl do and remember all the fine things she learn from her ma.'

"Then the pa sit many days at the loom and weave the gold thread into a fine cloth, and his heart is big with glad because the cloth is strong, and as he work he can no feel the hurt in his back because he say, 'The girl will be strong like the thread and can no break in any place, but every way she will be fine and neat.' Then the horn-bill come and say, 'So it be, if the girl remember the ways of her people.'

"When the girl came from the bush she dance past all the girls and when the shake-shake [calabash rattle] sing, her feet spin like the top, and her smile is bright like the sun, and the chief self say, 'I will take that girl to the mat [marry her].'

"When the ma give the cloth to the girl, the girl wrap it tight and she look fine. Then the hornbill come and say, 'This cloth you must always keep. It is made of the fine ways and the take-care of your people. When you wash it in the waterside, it no good to beat it hard on the rock, but let it fall softly-softly from your hand. Let nothing carry it from you.'

"But the girl get big-ways in the bush. She want civ-ilized thing. She can't care for country ways again. She run away from the chief and go to the coast. She say, 'I will be a free mamma [prostitute] and buy me fine things.' When she reach Monrovia, she go to the traders and buy American cloth and throw her country-cloth lappa in the waterside. The Neji reach up to take the fine cloth but it stay for the hand of the girl and she can no free her hand so the Neji carry the girl also. But when the girl stand before the chief in the Neji village under the river, they don' like that girl and they keep only the cloth and send the girl to the top of the water again, for only the cloth is fine. They say 'Leff the girl for the crocodiles to chop. Civilized ways do not belong to we.'

"And so it is that the country things be fine for coun-try people and belong to them, and the people must hold them tight and not throw them down. And sometimes civilized ways are good but they are not good just because they are different from country ways. And that, O Chief, is the story the old people tell the young ones when they want new thing because it is new, and not because they see it is good. And at night the old men look into the river and see the gold cloth shining under the water and they call the young ones to see."

Nya was silent a long time. Finally he said, "The story has sense, for true." The old women nodded, and everyone was very quiet. The silence was as great a tribute to Buno's storytelling as the loud ovation had been for Johnny's dancing. Nya rose and said "Wait small, Ma. Excuse, please," and went into his house. I walked among the seated women and looked for old beads while he was gone. When they understood what I wanted the headwife went to her hut and came back with several old glass beads which I think are Venetian.

"I have these from my ma," she said. "And my ma had them from her ma. I would not sell them to any person. But because the white ma has got good heart for old things, I dash you."

I took them reverently and touched them to my heart in the manner of the Mandingos. She nodded that she understood.

Nya came out of the house with a calabash of wild honey which he gave to me. I showed him the beads the headwife had given me, and asked Sendro to tell him that in the time when I had traveled many days on the water away from the face of my people, it was in part for beads like this that I had come.

"Those beads," Nya instructed Sendro to tell me, "have swam over much water and walked by land among many people for many years before they came to we. And it is good that now they live for the hand of the ma who has been brave over many Neji villages under the big water and walked for many days by land. The heart of the beads can lie down good in the hand of this ma, and our hearts lie down for the ma also."

"And now what thing you like from me for dash, O Chief, to hold tight the good-friend palaver?"

"Ma," Sendro told me, "the thing the chief wants is this: He says in the land of your people it must be that you are a great woman chief like Suokoko. He wants you to tell your people the things you see in his country. He does not know why it was that many rice-plantings before his own father, the people of your country sent the Liberian government people who take the land of his people. And he thinks the people of your country do not know the bad ways of the government people to the native man — the way they take the poor man's rice and chickens and goats, the way they come and break the village when they vex for small thing, the burning kerosene over the head when the tax it not paid, the loads that must be carried with no pay and no chop, the twenty-five [lashes] that fall so easy on the back, the boys that go for Fernando Po."

"Tell him, Sendro, that in the land of my people, my voice is small but that I will speak, and some will hear."

"For the glad that you put in the hearts of his people this day," Sendro told me, "it is the wish of the chief that he stand under the roof of your hammock and carry you from the town. This, Ma, is a thing I have never seen a chief do."

"*Bo-vo-ni-o* [Come, my hammock men]," I called, and the hammock men quickly strung my hammock under the frame, and I sat there with all the people watching while Johnny brought the dash chest and measured out the usual salt and kerosene.

The orchestra assembled in front of the hammock and behind the headwife who was to lead the procession. At a signal from Nya they began to play and he gravely ex-changed places with the man at my right shoulder. Nya stood spire-straight as though the weight of the frame touched him lightly or not at all. In this gesture of hu-mility he seemed more regal than when he had sat en-throned in a purple hammock surrounded by his wealth of toiling wives. It was I who had changed stature, not he, for I felt shamed that I knew no manifestation with which to meet the thing he had done.

We proceeded in a dusty swirl to the top of the high hill beyond the town, convoyed by all of the village, in-cluding the dogs. When we parted it was with repeated finger-snapping and loud good-byes in Mano and Kpuesi. The reiteration somehow made up for the lack of mutual vocabulary.

We started on down the trail. When I looked back, Nya was backing down the hill, holding aloft his red fez — not waving it, but just holding it in crimson salute. Sendro bounced along beside me waving his cow's-tail wand and blowing charcoal embers out of his little clay pipe, an indication that in his opinion the trek was go-ing exceedingly well.

CHAPTER TWENTY-TWO

Forest Fury

Sendro called me at three-thirty in the morning and said that we must start early because bad things were going to happen that day. His pipe was dead and he pulled with drooped lips at the stem. This meant that things were expected to be very bad indeed, to yield as little joy and comfort as the bitter pipe. He gave a speech to the carriers before we left and told the men that each must walk strong and hold himself tight, that it would be a day in which a weak stick might fall to the path and never rise to walk again.

It had rained in the night and the termites were flying. They dropped into the coffee Johnny had ready for me, tangled themselves in my hair, and fell down the neck of my shirt. The carriers started on ahead while Sendro sat on the ground waiting for me with his chin on his knees. Every line of his face expressed premonition of evil things about to descend upon us. I thought it was because he had not eaten the day before. He tapped the bowl of his pipe and the sound was brittle with futility. I fished termites out of coffee between gulps, and tried to hurry.

271

"All right, Sendro. I fini. Let go, yah? How far in front the men?"

"I send them in front the long time you sit to drink coffee, Ma. But sometime they can stop to chop bug-a-bug [termites]."

"You like bug-a-bug, Sendro?"

"Sure, Ma. He fine chop. But no time this bad day."

"What bad thing can catch we, Sendro?" Had he heard that there were bush cow on the trail? Would a Kpuesi devil be walking and try to stop us?

"Well, Ma, I can no say. But you will see. If all we live tonight, it be for the luck you carry."

"Let your heart lie down, Sendro. I carry fine medicine for trouble in this good gun I wear. If you fear, then let the man who carries the big gun walk behind me today."

"The gun is not medicine for the trouble that will catch we," Sendro predicted gloomily.

If the danger ahead were real, and not a thing of Sendro's sour imagining, would it not be better to stay in the village until the jungle were secured from the lurking evil? Sendro said it would not. The native does not know this kind of running away. He believes in a pattern and the pattern is larger than the individual or group of individuals. A condemned man will seldom flee his village. He might take refuge on the coast or on the plantation but this he will not do. The pattern that holds him has long fingers that can reach out to trip him on the trail. It is omnipresent. He can no more escape it than he can escape himself. He stays without visible chains and meets the irrevocable. Movement over the trail is the pattern of a safari. Sitting down to avoid meeting a moving evil is as unthinkable as running from a static one. We will move today. We will start early in order to meet and be done with the Thing as soon as possible and with morning strongness. Danger must not be met by bodies slack with fatigue. Foundering in gloom, but with the will clenched and the empty belly tight, Sendro will have us move ahead into the dark tunnel that is the path through the jungle.

The air was a heaviness through which to wallow the body forward, an evil sulphurous substance that could not be forced through the narrow channels of the nostrils but had to be gulped through the mouth and melted with body warmth before it could be swallowed. Termites fluttered and fell like snow. Their wings were scarcely more dense or white than the wraiths of fog which lapped at us with cold ghostly tongues. One's hand, brushed across the lips to rid the mouth of the gluey membranous wings, felt cold and bony as though that part of the body had died.

In the first village we overtook the carriers who had squatted around a fire, eating termites which a woman was frying in rancid palm oil. Sendro scooped up a handful of the grublike bodies, crisp with the hot oil, and scrunched them between his teeth before he scolded the men for stopping.

"We have no heart to walk through the bush this day without our ma," Buno said. "It is good we all stay close."

They helped each other hoist the loads to their heads. Quickly and without conversation, each man started

walking rapidly ahead as soon as his load weight was balanced. Sendro had no need to wave his cow's tail, nor to
boom, "Allez! Allez!" after them. They spurted down
the path like black slippery seeds squirted from the
thumb and finger of a hand they could feel but could
not see. They moved out of the village compound into
the funereal dankness of the jungle, and were swallowed
by the greenish fog, the light heel of the back foot swallowed last of all, moving silently like figures in a sinister
dream. My boot heels bruised the spongy moss of the
path and the squeak which Johnny had once admired
annoyed him now by its impertinence. It was a crickety
metronome, speeding up with my pace, slowing when I
slowed, ticking off the distance between ourselves and
doom, insinuating itself between the splitting fabric of
my nerves. The silence of the jungle, which usually
seems a holy thing, had been polluted. Before Johnny
had stopped talking altogether he had said that it was
on such a day as this that the twisted lianas hanging from
the trees turned into writhing pythons which reached out
and hooked grown men with their fangs before they
strangled and engulfed the limp bodies.

We walked for three hours before the patient jungle
rose in fury to shake itself from the grip of constricting
evil. The awful quiet was broken by a growl of wind. It
was not heard first as a distant roar approaching with
rain-burden; it seemed to originate out of the suddenly
churned place where we were. Leaves, branches, limbs
of trees sailed through the air, paper-light. The fury
mounted quickly. At first it seemed that thousands of
demons were in every tree, wrenching them apart, twist-

ing the limbs, ripping big branches, tearing off pieces of bark like flakes of old wallpaper from the white walls of the trunks.

I saw ahead of me through the littered air a great cotton tree and made my way toward it as best I could, hoping to find shelter in the cove of high buttresses. When I had almost reached it, beating against the wind and panting, there was a tearing sound as the roots ripped from the ground and with a great crash it fell across the path in front of me, carrying lesser trees to the earth in its wake.

Then it seemed that this was not a thing of demons wresting the trees from without but that every leaf and branch and trunk were possessed from within, that the writhing forest was in an agony of battle with all the forces in the earth. It was wild and beautiful. I had felt this way once at a Wagner opera, but then I was outside the turmoil watching as from another planet. Now I was in it, part of it, part of the wildness and beauty and pain and violence of this weird passion of the forest. That I was not afraid had nothing to do with courage. It was simply that while I was part of it, I could not fear it.

For the first time in my life, I felt that I understood a little of what death may be like, a becoming one with the mighty forces that move through the universe. And if sometime the force which now is I were to be blended with these other forces, it is in such wild beauty as this that I should like to move.

I have no idea how long the forest was rent. Eventually the rain came so thickly that I could not see the trees that blocked my path until I struck them with my body. I was so cold that I had to grope my way forward, had to keep moving.

Behind me, I could hear above the roar of the wind and rain what might have been the crying of my carriers or the whine of branches scraping against each other. Some of the men must have been caught under falling trees. Sendro would know what to do better than I. I pushed on to Gbonga. The wind slapped my soaked clothes against me, streams of cold water ran out of my hair, my arm was swelling where a flying branch had grazed it. Now the beauty of the storm was spent I felt altogether miserable and depleted. The forest had grappled in splendid might with the evil which had filtered through it. Many giants had fallen but the air was thin again and good to breathe. The rain slackened and stopped.

The jungle seemed immensely clean, with a cleanliness beyond that of the slashing wash of rain. It filled now with fresh quiet, settling layer upon layer like fallen leaves. The silence of jungle after a storm is so immense that it seems a thing of substance with weight and sheen and color of mauve shadows on fruiting moss under overhanging rocks. The dimensions of this Silence are beyond those of the jungle, higher than the leaf-frilled ceiling, deeper into the soil than the roots of the trees, and wide and long beyond many days of march.

I was glad to see that on the hill ahead the two big trees which are the pillared gateway of Gbonga were still standing. As I passed under them and stood on the cleared earth of the town, the dark battle clouds which roofed the sky parted before the golden shafts of a vigorous sun.

I knocked at many closed doors of the huts of Gbonga,

but none would open to me, nor make any answer to my calls. Every window was shuttered, every door latched while the people huddled together, not sure that the evils of the day were past. I remembered that there was a Catholic mission in the town, though I did not know whether there were nuns, nor how many people in the group. I saw a spacious building and a large compound on a little hill at the end of one of the winding streets. I would go there and ask for shelter.

My knock was answered by an old man wearing priest's clothing. His face was of the pallor and translucence of an altar candle and set with large eyes which were bright and soot-black. His beard fell far down on his chest and was loosely wavy as though it had just been combed. It was like calling for help and having one of the ancient prophets step out of the Old Testament in answer to your cry.

"I do not wish to embarrass you by coming to your

house alone," I said with chattering teeth, "but all my carriers are behind and I do not know what has happened to them in the storm. If I may, I would like to go to your kitchen to get warm and dry."

"Nonsense, child. You do not embarrass me. This is Africa! Come in." His voice was deep and rolling with Irish lilts in it. "It is a good wind that blows you here. I have not talked to an educated person for many days. It may be that I have forgotten the ways of talk. Go to the kitchen by the fire while I rummage around and find an outfit of clothes for you, and then we will have tea." It was as though he had said, "Come in, world."

I followed a houseboy through a covered runway to the kitchen where a wood fire was roaring in a clay stove.

"Father was about to have tea?" I asked, seeing that the teakettle was breaking out steam from the spout.

"Missy, the steward for Father has always the water ready to roll in a vex for tea. If not so, the hot steam is from the mouth of the Father, and that is not good."

The priest called me when he had assembled an outfit of his clothing, complete except for socks.

"Every sock I own is full of holes," he said ruefully. "You take these things into the room there and get into them and I'll rummage the cupboard in the hall for socks. I thought I had a new pair. . . ."

I put on the long cotton underwear which was the kind my grandfather used to wear, and buttoned it up to my throat. The crisp clean feel of a white shirt with too much cassava starch in it! The encasing warmth of a pair of trousers around chilled legs! The coldness of the concrete floor under bare feet!

"Let me darn your socks while I wait for the carriers," I said. "I would like to do it!"

We sat in the long, bare living room. There was a square table and four chairs in one end and a water filter set on a beautifully carved and painted blue box. The box and a picture of Christ were the only adornment in the spare, oblong cell.

"It would be good to see a woman's hands moving with a thread and needle, in the way of my mother's hands making our clothing," he said. "But then your attention would be for your work, and I am anxious to hear how things are in the world. So, let us talk. Tea will be ready in a minute. What of the war?"

"I have been away from home for two months myself so I'm afraid I can't bring you up to date, Father."

"News that is only two months old is brand-new to me," he said.

I did most of the talking. When we had finished discussing the war, he seemed to be content with sharing silence rather than conversation. We had tea sitting at the table which was covered with Irish linen. A yellow quilted tea cozy covered the teapot.

"My mother made it for me," he said. "She was a wonderful lady!"

"Is she still living? Will you see her when you go on leave?"

"She is living," he said. "But who can say that she will be when leave comes? I have been here seven years now. We can't get replacements at present and there are many of the Fathers who need a change of climate worse than I. I don't think about leave."

"But you must have had fever, many times?"

"I have it all the time, but I keep it down enough to get around as long as the quinine lasts. A few months ago my supply ran out and I had a bad bout."

"Tell me about your home in Ireland," I said.

"It is very green in Ireland," he said. "But it is not the same kind of green as Africa. It is soft and gentle and new-looking. You know how grass looks in the morning in the spring when the dew sparkles on it? The heavy green of the jungle is like a witch's brew in comparison. We lived in a little cottage, and my mother . . . "

He was silent again, staring into his tea while it grew cold.

"That beautiful box," I said, "did you make it?"

He did not hear me at first, and then realizing that I had spoken, he was confused and I was sorry I had broken the silence.

"Forgive me," he said, pouring more tea for me. "It has been so long since I have had anyone to talk to that I am still alone even though you are here. For months I have craved to have a guest and now that I have one, I have forgotten how to talk. After you have gone, my tongue will loosen with all the things I will be wanting to ask you after it is too late."

"Why don't you come to the plantation for a vacation, Father?"

"My work is here and there is so much to be done! Time is precious. I can't squander it by resting myself. And now about the box. There was a Father here before me who made it. He was clever enough to be able to

refresh himself with color and whenever he could get a
little paint he made things like that box. He built this
house, and you can see that though it is plain and simple,
there was much care in the choice of wood that went into
this ceiling, and into the making of the doors. He liked
the termite tracks in wood for the ceiling. He said that
the vermiculations were the sculpture of living creatures."

I looked at a shadow moving past the window. Sendro
was coming to the door, his clay pipe under full steam.
I knew by this, before I asked him, that no one had died
in the storm.

"How the men, Sendro?"

He came into the living room, dripping a puddle of
water on the concrete floor. He stooped nearly double as
he entered, a sign of humility in entering the home of an
esteemed person.

"Ma, they all right. A bush caught one man in a way
that is very bad for a man to be caught." He squatted
his knees and fumbled in his groin to show me how it
had been with the injured one.

"Can he walk, Sendro, or he stay for the path?"

"He can walk now, Ma. I make medicine for him."
The glowing ember in the pipe swelled into rubescent
flame.

"First, the man lay on the ground and cry. But I say
to him, 'No mind, yah? I can tailor you into a man again.'
So, I take needle, I take thread from Ma's black box that
Johnny carry. And I close shut like so [sewing motions]
the place that lay open."

"But the hurt must catch the man hard, Sendro."

"Well, Ma, I think so, but the man do' care for hurt. He never cry after I start to tailor him. The thing he cry for first time no be the hurt; it be because he think he can no make pickin again. But now he fine."

"Someone can carry his load?"

"So I tell him, Ma. But he say, 'No, I am a *man*; I can carry my load!'"

"I will give you rice and dry wood," said the Father, "and by the time your men all get here, Sendro can have their chop ready for them. Meanwhile, let's have some more tea."

The carriers draggled in, one behind the other. The contents of all the cases were soaked, except the clothing in one tin trunk. They were cheerful about their bruises and scratches, displaying them to me proudly. One of them rubbed ashes into a gash across his face.

"Why you do that thing?" I asked.

"Ma," he said, "if the hurt stay big, the people in the camp on the plantation will believe me when I tell them the hellova thing we see today."

While the men ate we looked at the schoolhouse the Father had built and at the flowering shrubs in the compound. Caladium, waxy white as calla lilies, shot its flowers above large, rippling, color-spotted leaves. "The red and white spots on those green leaves are where the Creator spattered his twig paintbrush clean when he finished painting the jungle plants," the Father said. "At least that is the native belief."

"Tell me," I said, "do these boys in your school really

learn to read, Father, and is the effort worth all you are giving to it of your strength?"

"They learn to read rather quickly," he said. "You see they understand symbols and as soon as they get the idea that words are symbols of ideas, they are pathetically eager to learn. A person cannot know the taste of a thing he has never tried on his tongue. There are many ideas that are like untasted food to these boys, and those words are difficult for them. Sacrifice they can understand, because they have experienced it in their pagan rites. Words for things come to them easily. Words for *ideas* acquire meaning only as they are explained in terms of the nearest thing to it in their experience. These things have to be built up through generations of teaching."

Sendro was eager to be off. "There are two ways to go from Gbonga, Ma," he said. "One is the way you came, through Suokoko. The other is through big bush and land of some Kpuesi people with bad ways. In the land of the bad Kpuesi there is only one village. That way the path is cool on the feet and the way is short past the other way. If Ma agree, we like to go that way, but it is necessary to start just now or dark can catch we on the trail."

"Let us go through the land of the big bush, then, Sendro. The men have seen much to carry their strength today and I do not think the bad Kpuesi can be bad too much to we."

"These Kpuesi people are very dirty, Ma, and they never take care to build town fine, so it may be Ma will have to sleep in a poor house."

Each of the men filed past the priest and thanked him for the rice and fire as they left the Mission. I found some tins of food to leave for my dash.

"I am glad for this," said the Father. "I do not take sufficient care for my food. And now I would like to give you the box you admired so much."

It was one of the only two spots of color in the living room. I couldn't possibly accept it! I was more moved than when the native families had tried to give me children. I could not answer at once.

"When I remember this afternoon," I said finally, "there are three things that I shall like to think of as surrounding you. One is the Irish linen cloth on your table, and one is the tea cozy your mother quilted, and the other is that painted box. It will belong to me more by leaving it here with you than by my carrying it. You see it is a part of the picture I carry of your hospitality and it would be violating the picture, like cutting away part of a snapshot, if I took it."

He seemed to understand. "It is only a thing," he said, "and it is not right for me to care too much for things."

When I hear or read the word "hospitality," the picture I see in my mind is a blue box, with the grain of the wood showing through like the light threads of worn blue denim, adorned by primitively painted red flowers that could grow only in nostalgia which had its roots in Ireland.

We walked rapidly through the short hilarious afternoon. The jungle birds set the forest trilling with song.

The veda (or whidah) birds hovered over the path, the male using this space for his ardent wooing. His courting is a dance in the air before the female, and his drooping tail feathers, which in the breeding season are twice the length of his body, flit like footless limbs in a small space. He resembles the artificial birds on sticks which whirr at the end of strings at carnivals. The hornbills roared like starting locomotives, and the monkeys sassed them back in querulous treble. The boys tried to drown out all the other sounds by singing amplified accounts of the storm. Women hurried from Gbonga to their farms, carrying produce. It was one of the rare times in the tropics when nothing is languid or sluggish.

By trotting when we were not walking, we reached the Kpuesi town just before dark. The drums were playing and the people danced in circles grouped all over the compound. It was as though a mosaic design of circles had started to flow in their setting, keeping their design while they moved. The chief was drunk with cane juice and there was no way to make him understand my need for a house.

"I think, Ma, that the way we can manage is to put your hammock in the palaver house," Sendro said. "We will build small fires and the men will sleep on the floor so nothing bad can catch you in the hammock."

The men stacked their loads in a circle around the palaver house and lay on the floor. The shed was large but we were too many people. Some of their legs overflowed across the edge of the small ledge that bounded the shelter. They slept with their heads toward the small fires they built, their bodies radiating like sticks of wood.

I could watch the dancing from where I lay in the hammock strung between two poles. A small fire cast a grotesque shadow-drummer against the wall of a hut. The shadow-man threw back his mammoth head and heaved his shoulders with the rhythm, a genie grown out of the pounded drum. When the chief finally collapsed

in a sodden heap, some of his men carried him to his hut and the dancing ceased with the drumming. The circles flowed into lines that separated before the doors of huts, and the village slept. Sendro would not lie down with the men but dozed with his back against the pole to which the hammock was tied.

"These are bad people, Ma. I sit here the whole night so nothing can catch our ma."

The moon shone straight into the village compound. The night was soft and delicate. The need to see its beauty was greater than the need to sleep. The idea of sleeping seemed like thinking of Sunday dinner during a prayer. On the floor the little fires died into faint embers. With their last flickerings they made great shadows of the grotesque tangle of arms and legs of the sleeping men. I was less alien to my sleeping carriers than the people of their own color inside the huts a few feet away. We were one unit, a small tribe, taking risks together, trusting each other, looking to each other for security and protection. A great tenderness welled up within me for these strong men to whom I was *Ma*.

In the morning when the village people began to stir, I greeted them in Kpuesi but they made no response.

"These people cannot hear our kind of Kpuesi, Ma," Buno explained. "They cannot hear me, and Ma and I talk the same way."

The latter was overstatement, but Buno was proud that what little I knew of his language I had learned from him. He had taught me patiently as though I were a child while I missed the inflections and tonal variations.

When I came back from a small walk into the jungle the villagers ran to the place where I had gone.

"Why do the people do that, Buno?"

"Well, Ma, every part of a person is that person even after it leaves him, you see. If the chop that Ma eat yesterday is left in the bush just now the people will take away the leaves to find that part, and make strong medicine from it."

"What kind of medicine?"

"Medicine to be strong like the ma, medicine to grow long hair like the ma, medicine to have much money like the ma, medicine for luck, the medicine for shoot meat, the medicine for dance in the water [swim] without the Neji catch the leg."

"How can the people know these things be part me? We make no talk."

"Ma, you do' hear the drums talk when we leave Gbonga yesterday? Plenty people know plenty thing about the white ma that never put eye on her."

CHAPTER TWENTY-THREE

Firestone Ma

T HE DAY BEFORE we reached Salala I told Sendro that I thought we should send the strongest walker ahead with a note to the plantation, so that my husband could come for me and I would not have to ride the shilling bus. I wanted no more of "And-So-What," nor his transportation.

We decided which boy should be messenger and I wrote a note while the men ate rice at a roadside kitchen. A native woman cooked it for them, stirring the rounded bottom of the clay pot by whirling an anchor-shaped stick between her palms. The bottom of the anchor was the exact curve of the bottom of the pot. This kitchen was the nearest thing I had seen to a restaurant in Liberia.

When we explained to the boy what we wanted him to do, he looked apologetic and refused.

"Tell him he can see dash for this, Sendro."

"Ma, he never come to the coast before, and he ashamed for he not got coat, and the people tell him that all the people here wear coat."

"You mean trouser, Sendro?"

"No, Ma, it be coat-part he talk. He say big man wear coat every time."

"Give him your singlet, then. I can get a new one for you at the plantation."

Sendro took off the undershirt he was wearing and gave it to the man. There were so many holes in it he did not get his head through the one intended for that purpose. He was short and the singlet sagged almost to his knees. He pulled it up tight around his waist, gathered the excess material into a big knot over his stomach, and saluted in the manner of a Frontier Force soldier.

"O.K., Ma. I go now."

My messenger was off at a stiff pace, his naked behind very black beneath the comparatively white singlet.

When we passed the Polish Plantation, the boys felt they were almost home and Johnny made up a song in English:

> The Missy goes for Salala; the Missy goes for Salala,
> Today is the day-o for boss to buy the chicken-egg,
> So wait in Salala, boss, wait in Salala!
> We coming boss, we coming, so wait in Salala!

Johnny said his left foot told him that the master was in Salala at that moment. Buno was so impressed by Johnny's prophetic extremity that he broke into a run. When I asked Johnny what his right foot said he answered, "The right foot say, 'Left foot, you lie.' "

The left foot was right. By dusk the cases were loaded on the back of the pickup and the plantation boys were sitting on them like conquering heroes on thrones. Johnny was telling the other boys that as soon as he got home he would organize a travel club, and of course he would be the president because no other Bassau boy had ever gone to the French boundary and come back alive. He was quite a different Johnny from the cringing little boy who had hung onto my wrist after dark when we walked in the Kpuesi country.

"How did you know I was here?" I asked Bob. "My messenger couldn't have reached you so soon."

"Poor Boy told me last night that you would arrive today. When I asked him what time, he said he would tell me the hour tomorrow. Right after lunch he got me up from my nap and told me it was time to start. I heard the drums talking in the camp last night. I suppose he had it from them, though he would not say."

The carriers formed into a straight line and I paid them off (after getting additional money from Bob as is always the way when I come back from safari). Sixpence for each man for each day, and then a sixpence dash for each. Then down the line again, snapping fingers with each man and telling him good-bye in Mano, careful to give the same word of praise to each. Elephant-hoof bracelets and wooden bracelets and leopard teeth came off their arms for dash for me. Each of them said "Ma" as we parted.

Sendro left me with a burst of oratory, during which the carriers broke their formal line and gathered around us. I presented Sendro to Bob when the speech was over, and he put aside his pipe as he said, "All right; I now give the Ma into your care." This was deliberate, and after a long frank scrutiny of my husband, as though he were making up his mind whether or not he were leaving me in good hands.

Cool polished floors, ice clinking in tall glasses, servants rolling on the green grass in glee because the Missy had come home, Bwi Smalldog refusing to lie anywhere except on my feet, Sa the mongoose crawling up the skirt of my evening dress and cuddling like a fur piece around my neck, the gramophone playing and the planters asking for dances, the travelers' palm rustling outside the windows, the sun going down behind Research Hills! Why do I leave this clean lovely place to go off in the bush?

I remember the sting of salty perspiration in my eyes, the saw grass slashing my clothes and skin, the vines and roots that seem alive, reaching out to tear and trip, the insects that bite, the rain, everlasting rain. . . .

I look out over the purpling hills; I wonder what the far one is like, and the one beyond that, and then a vision of the whole continent of Africa spreads out in my mind like a relief map. Far beyond the hills I have climbed are the Sangha Cliffs, and beyond that, over in Timbuktu, is aging Father Yokuba sitting on a roof top drinking Pernod and grumbling at the mountainous black Salome for whom he gave up the church. Perched on the edge of the desert is the walled city of Kano whose textiles I must see; and in the vast beyond are the Great Rift and the Mountains of the Moon. . . . Mountains of the Moon. . . . In the camp the drums are tuning up. The moon turns the yellow-green palm fronds to blue green and silver. The drums grow louder, the soles of my feet ache. Mountains of the Moon . . .

Several weeks after I returned from Ganta, we heard

that Chief Nya Qua was expected in Kakata. We went to
greet him and to get some of the leopard teeth he had
promised me.

"Nya Qua, this be my man." I presented my husband.

Nya looked Bob over carefully. "You got fine woman,"
he said. "How much you pay for her?"

"Oh, Chief, that woman cost me plenty-o," Bob assured the chief. "I never finish pay for her this time. All
my life, I pay, I pay, I can't finish pay. But, she fine for
true."

"Fine for true," echoed Nya who sat appraising me,
and spat a stream of cola to make it emphatic. "How
many women you buy, goo' friend?"

"This my one-part wife."

"Shame palaver!" Nya swung his head from side to
side. "I got plenty women, too many. Here, I dash you
this one."

He spoke to a woman sitting in a hammock. She rose
and grinned, took Bob's arm, and gestured toward the
door of the house.

"I sorry, Chief. I no fit to take the fine dash." Bob's
face, flushing to the brim of his helmet, was more than I
could endure without laughing.

"How you no fit, goo' friend? You be young man and
this woman fine-o. Not so? You like one other, maybe?"
He made a sweeping gesture that included the entire
retinue.

Bob spoke through an interpreter now, very careful to
make his meaning clear.

"Tell the chief that the woman is fine, and all his

wives are fine for true. But my one wife she can make palaver for me. Oh, Chief, that woman can vex! You know what a palaver a woman can make, oh, Chief?"

"Aye, goo' friend, I know the hellova palaver a woman can make." Nya spoke to the woman in Kpuesi and she released her clutch on Bob's arm. "Aye, goo' friend, I know women ways."

Nya Qua and Bob exchanged sympathetic glances.

CHAPTER TWENTY-FOUR

Gwiwoolio

W E HAD GONE to bed late and were on the fringe of sleep when a messenger threw pebbles against the window.

"There is a Clipper leaving tomorrow. Be at the airport at eight." The message had a nightmare quality.

"It is impossible," I said. "We have planned on several more weeks. We are not packed. Besides, we have called a party for the week-end; the guests are all invited!"

We were at the airport at eight!

We had called the servants into the living room and told them they must spend the remainder of the night helping us pack.

"Poor Boy," my husband said, "light a lantern. Get your Buzi sword. Go to the house of my secretary, Aiken, and tell him to go to the office. It is necessary for me to write paper until morning. You and the others must help the Missy plenty because I cannot myself stay here to help her."

At first there were blank stares. The news had not

penetrated the fog of their sleep-drug. Johnny was the first to understand.

"Missy you mean to say you go to your country to-morrow?"

"Yes, Johnny, that is the meaning." My words sounded to me as though someone else had said them.

A long cry like a funeral wail broke from his throat. Then the others took it up, a treble wail of grief. They lay on the floor and rolled from side to side as they cried.

"There is no time to cry," I shouted. "Put your feet under you! Myself, I cry in my heart, but there is much work to be done before my cry can come out."

My voice was unheard in the din. Poor Boy brought the lantern and his hand shook as he struck a match. Tears blinded him. I took the lantern and my hand trembled the flame from the third match before the wick took fire. Then I saw Poor Boy run out into the night, the yellow light casting a golden glow against his white trouser legs as he bobbed along. It was December, the Devil Moon, when no native boy walks alone on the road at night even with a torch and a sword. Yet Poor Boy, who knew that the hunters of human hearts were abroad for their strength-medicine, went off alone without a word.

I looked at my husband across the prostrate wailing boys rocking their heads against their knees.

"I might as well send them under the house so you won't have to step over them," Bob said. "They won't be of any use tonight."

Poor Boy was back in a few minutes, his eyes great rolling orbs of terror.

"Massio, Aiken refuse to come out of his house without a white man call him. He say when one black man call another from his door in the month of the Devil Moon, it be to take his heart from his body."

"All right, Poor Boy. I can go for him in the motor car. Thank you for going on the road for me. Now you get all the boys downstairs so the Missy can walk quick-time through the house."

The next few hours were a blur of bureau drawers being dumped in the middle of the floor, clothing tangled in silverware, carving tools and cooking pots, unfinished paintings, crocodile skins, guns, leopard pelts, and boots, evening dresses, underwear, books, and Victrola records. . . .

Every loved, used article piled on the floor brought floods of memories tearing through me until I was full and bursting with them, but still, I could not cry. The memories ran down my mind like a cascading waterfall tumbling over itself in its descent. There were the kerosene crates which had gone ahead of me so many trails, the fire-branded initials with the backward S still black on the sides.

The growing heap in the middle of the floor was a mound of things I wanted to hold separately in my hands. It seemed a pyre of all I had done or wanted to do in Africa.

I had yet to figure the servants' accounts. One pound, four charged against Poor Boy. That was the time he had to buy his Branca a new lappa and "talk sweet-mouth" to her to keep her from carrying little Monday-man and going to visit her people while the rivers were high. . . . Two and six charged against Johnny. That was to pay for the time he had vexed with a Bassau girl and called her a slave. The two and six was hush money to keep her from suing him. . . . Five shillings charged against Yagbo. That was for the new white headcloth his mother needed when she had become a "Bible woman" at the Lutheran Mission.

"*Gwiwoolio* [My face goes from you now]!" It is always a sad thing to say. This time I would say it from the air, and not from the crest of the third hill beyond the end of the motor road leading toward the interior.

"Gwiwoolio." I hold my heart tight.

At four o'clock, the mountain of things in the middle of the floor seemed higher than ever although many boxes had been packed and nailed shut. Pickups started arriving, the news of our sudden leaving having covered the plantation in the strange way that news travels in Africa.

The dashes were still to be attended to — one of my bright colored blouses to each of the servants, a long pair of Bob's white duck trousers to Poor Boy because he had cared for them so well and looked at them so wistfully, the unused Chore Girls to Johnny because he loved to wear the coppery pom-poms in his hair, the glasses to be divided among the Farmington planters because they had drunk from them so many toasts to friendship.

I went under the house and shook Sammi. He blinked through tear-swollen eyes.

"One last thing to do for the Missy, Sammi," I said.

"All our good friends come for good-byes. Make one pot full of strong coffee. Clean papaya. Make all the bread that remain into toast with cinnamon on top. One big bacon with the tar still around it stay for the chop cupboard. Cut all in thin slices and fry."

"So I do for you, Missy. Come, Johnny! Dress table, man!"

One last breakfast at the big table.

One last finger-snapping.

"Missy, can I have this one?" Buno appeared with an old aluminum water pitcher full of dents and minus the handle.

"Of course, but why you want that one? Water cannot stay inside again."

"You see this one?" he said, pointing to the largest of the many dents. "My head made that one. The time I put pepper in the eyes of the small boy, you hit me over the head, Missy, to learn me sense. This the place where sense leave your hand for my head."

What one says in good-byes are not the words of the heart. Even "gwiwoolio" and "salaam alaikum" do not put into sound the ache and the sense of loss. Good-byes are felt in heart-hurt through many months after the futile words are said which mark the moment of parting.

Supper in Africa, breakfast in Brazil! Ahead, New York, department stores, malted milk, and head lettuce!

I looked down on the clouds that were like the rolls of cotton Sahda had taught me to card.

Now, I thought, I know how Whitman felt when he wrote, "I inhale great draughts of space!"

Attendants fumigated the Clipper for mosquitoes at every stop, but they cannot fumigate from the great bird-machine the feeling of the strange lands she has cast away from her in many risings. When you have been borne away on the strong wings from a land you have loved, you have not left that land behind! The meanings of the things you have experienced have become part of you, even as bone and tissue. You hug every memory close to you keeping it alive. You walk the streets, and concrete bruises the soles of your feet. Then you leave the pavement and walk again on the spongy coolness of a forest path. You are pressed close by towering buildings, and you refute them for the huge living pillars of the forest. Your ears are battered by telephone jangle and traffic roar, and you close them for the hush of the jungle just before dawn breaks. You are jolted and lost in the intricacies of the subways and remember a land where the wheel had no significance. You see the native boys carrying clay on their heads in an inverted wheelbarrow, the wheel a useless spoked form against the sky. You listen to your friends talking, and their terrible concern about *things,* and you long for the pauses in native conversation where the animals and the wind speak great truths.

You are restless and disturbed and you know that this is the price which has to be paid for the happiness you have gathered from the swamps and hills and trails and people of a land that has become part of you.

This alien land is the one that has given you birth. Though you love it, and are proud of it, and are hurt by its confusions, there can be no singing in your heart at first. You know that before there can be song again, you must learn how to incorporate all you have experienced away from it into a new pattern of thinking and feeling.

The people on the streets in New York all seemed to be wearing a set mask of facial muscles. Only the children had the open faces of natives.

Why don't we, in this country, I thought, wear our spirits on our faces, and save the inscrutable to be carved in stone and wood?

I gravitated toward a group of children who had their noses pressed against the glass of Macy's Christmas windows. The mothers who had them in tow looked away in a bored manner and tapped their galoshes in the cold pavement. Inside the windows, a fat Santa Claus raised his spherical red-velveted behind over a moving sleigh full of glittering packages. Then a Christmas tree hung with shiny baubles moved across the window on a concealed track. Oh, beautiful shining baubles! When I was a child, I thought that Christmas baubles were packed tight with happiness, that they could explode like fireworks, and when they did all those beneath the falling, iridescent fragments would have some of the released happiness to hold forever. The Christmas tree moved on to the next window, all the baubles still intact.

Sufficient time has elapsed since then for me to see the strange land of Africa with some perspective. I have no patent answer for its many problems. I only know that the wealth of the country is not in the things that white men, since the days of the Portuguese sailing ships, have gone there to find — gold, ivory, pepper, slaves, rubber. The real wealth is in the intrinsic fineness and the amazing culture of the native tribesmen.

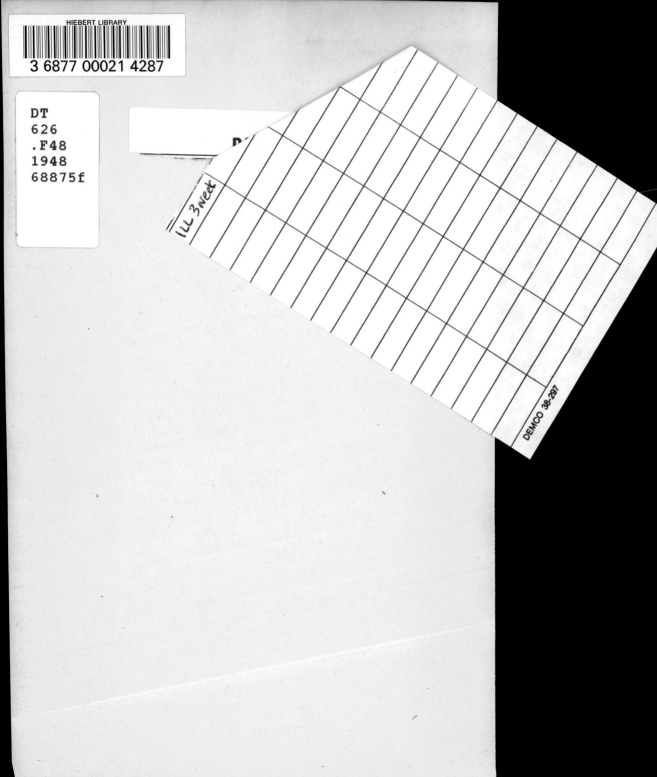

ILL 3 week

DEMCO 38-297